WHAT THE BIBLE TEACHES ABOUT HOMOSEXUALITY

A RESPONSE TO REVISIONIST, PRO-LGBTQI+ THEOLOGY

TELLER BOOKS

What the Bible Teaches About Homosexuality: A Response to Revisionist, Pro-LGBTQI+ Theology

© 2022 by TellerBooks™. All rights reserved. No part of this publication may be reproduced or transmitted in any form or by any means, including photocopying, recording, or copying to any storage and retrieval system, without express written permission from the copyright holder.

Cover art, "Sodom and Gomorrah," © 2010 by W. David Lilley, Jr. Used with permission.

ISBN (13) (Paperback): 978-1-68109-101-3
ISBN (10) (Paperback): 1-68109-101-1
ISBN (13) (ePub): 978-1-68109-102-0
ISBN (10) (ePub): 1-68109-102-X

LogosLight™
an imprint of TellerBooks™
TellerBooks.com/LogosLight

www.TellerBooks.com

Manufactured in the U.S.A.

NOTE: Unless otherwise stated herein, all biblical Scriptures quoted herein are taken from the New King James Version or American Standard Version translations, unless the verses are quoted directly from the Rev. Dr. White's book, in which case other translations may be used.

DISCLAIMER: The opinions, views, positions and conclusions expressed in this volume reflect those of the individual author and not necessarily those of the publisher or any of its imprints, editors or employees.

ABOUT THE IMPRINT

The mission of LogosLight™ is to reintroduce time-tested values and truths to modern debates on political, economic, and moral issues. The imprint focuses on books and monographs dealing with society, ethics, and public policy.

Contents

About the Imprint 3
Contents 5
Abbreviations 9

CHAPTER 1. INTRODUCTION 13

CHAPTER 2. THE HUMAN RIGHTS CAMPAIGN'S TEACHINGS ON HOMOSEXUALITY 15

CHAPTER 3. HOMOSEXUALITY: NOT A SIN, NOT A SICKNESS? 18

    A. Overview 18

    B. Sodom and Gomorrah's Sins were not Related to Homosexuality 18

    C. Christians Cannot Judge Homosexuality because They Do Not Follow the Old Testament Law 25

    D. Leviticus Was Intended to Prohibit "Idolatry"; the Reference to Homosexuality is Due to Mistranslation 27

    E. Christians are No Longer Bound by Biblical Law 30

    F. Romans 1:26-28 Does Not Condemn Homosexuality between Loving, Committed Partners 32

    G. Romans 1:26 Does Not Condemn Lesbianism; It Condemns Women Who Play a Dominant Role in Heterosexual Relationships 34

    H. "Homosexuals" in 1 Corinthians 6:9 Is a Mistranslation 35

    I. There Is "No Law against Love" 36

    J. Insights from Other Bible Scholars 37

CHAPTER 4. DOES THE SCRIPTURE AFFIRM THE LGBTQ COMMUNITY? 45

   A. God Loves LGBTQ People 45

   B. God Did not Make a Mistake in Creating LGBTQ People 46

   C. Being LGBTQ is not a Sin, but If It Were, It Would Be Forgiven 47

   D. The Idea of Multiple Gender Variants in the Bible 49

   E. Bible Verses that Have Been Used to Condemn LGBTQ People 51

CHAPTER 5. WHAT THE BIBLE SAYS—AND DOESN'T SAY—ABOUT HOMOSEXUALITY 69

   A. Introduction 69

   B. Misunderstanding the Divine Inspiration of the Scriptures 70

   C. The Old Testament Law as Inapplicable to Modern Society 72

   D. The Bible: a Book About God or "Human Sexuality"? 76

   E. Homosexuality Is Also Banned in the New Testament 78

CHAPTER 6. CONCLUSION 85

ANNEX 1. BIBLICAL VERSES DISCUSSING HOMOSEXUALITY 86

1. **GENESIS 19:5-8** 86

2. **LEVITICUS 18:22** 86

3. **LEVITICUS 20:13** 86

4. **JUDGES 19:20-25** 86

5. **ROMANS 1:26-28** 87

6. 1 CORINTHIANS 6:9-10 87

7. 1 TIMOTHY 1:9-11 88

ABBREVIATIONS

English Translations of the Bible:

ASV	American Standard Version
BBE	Bible in Basic English
Darby	Darby Bible
ESV	English Standard Version
ISV	International Standard Version
KJV	King James Version
MKJV	Modern King James Version
NIV	New International Version
NKJV	New King James Version
RSV	Revised Standard Version

Books of the Bible:

1Ch	1 Chronicles
1Co	1 Corinthians
1Jn	1 John
1Ki	1 Kings
1Pe	1 Peter
1Sa	1 Samuel
1Th	1 Thessalonians
1Ti	1 Timothy
2Ch	2 Chronicles
2Co	2 Corinthians
2Jn	2 John
2Ki	2 Kings
2Pe	2 Peter
2Sa	2 Samuel
2Th	2 Thessalonians
2Ti	2 Timothy
3Jo	3 John
Acts	Book of Acts
Amos	Book of Amos
Col	Colossians
Dan	Daniel
Deu	Deuteronomy

Ecc	Ecclesiastes
Eph	Ephesians
Est	Esther
Exo	Exodus
Eze	Ezekiel
Ezr	Book of Ezra
Gal	Galatians
Gen	Genesis
Hab	Habakkuk
Hag	Haggai
Heb	Hebrews
Hos	Hosea
Isa	Isaiah
Jas	James
Jer	Jeremiah
Job	Book of Job
Joel	Book of Joel
John	Gospel of John
Jon	Jonah
Jos	Joshua
Jude	Book of Jude
Jdg	Judges
Lam	Lamentations
Lev	Leviticus
Luke	Gospel of Luke
Mal	Malachi
Mark	Gospel of Mark
Mat	Gospel of Matthew
Mic	Micah
Nah	Nahum
Neh	Nehemiah
Num	Numbers
Oba	Obadiah
Phm	Philemon
Php	Philippians
Pro	Proverbs
Psa	Psalms
Rev	Revelation
Rom	Romans
Ruth	Book of Ruth

Son ....Song of Solomon
Tit....................Titus
Zec...................Zechariah
Zep ....Zephaniah

CHAPTER 1. INTRODUCTION

A growing number of commentators, including both scholars and even self-proclaimed Christians—have espoused the teaching that the Bible is either silent on the question of homosexuality, or, where it is not silent, it embraces, tolerates and accepts homosexuals and the homosexual lifestyle. While there are some accounts in the Bible such as the story of Sodom and Gomorrah or the law given in Leviticus 18:22 that have historically been viewed as prohibiting homosexuality, the revisionists teach that these verses in fact say nothing about homosexuality. They have been mistranslated, misquoted or misunderstood. In fact, the Bible teaches us to embrace the full spectrum of sexual orientations, so they say. The loving God who inspired the Bible allows sexual relations between same-sex couples and permits transgenderism and bisexuality within the context of loving, committed relationships.

Some Christian revisionists go a step further. They concede that the Old Testament in fact prohibited homosexuality, but the prohibitions of the Old Testament law have no place in the new covenant of grace, and therefore should have little bearing on the conduct of contemporary Christians. As for the apparent prohibitions of homosexual conduct in the New Testament, these are mostly based on mistranslations that misunderstand the original text. The term "homosexual" used in Paul's Epistles has no modern English equivalent, and is best rendered as the sexual exploitation of "effeminate call boys," not homosexual relations between two men or two women in committed, loving relationships.

It is not a narrow segment of Christians who embrace this revisionist theology. Many mainstream Protestant churches have embraced these teachings in droves. Prominent intellectuals at leading divinity schools, including at Harvard, Princeton and Yale, embrace this theology, rejecting traditional teachings on heterosexual, monogamous marriage in favor of unions between any and all people, regardless of their gender, sex or sexual orientation.

Revisionist church leaders and intellectuals have offered abundant arguments advocating for the abandonment of traditional teachings on marriage as outdated and based on historic prejudices. This book stands as a refutation and response to the revisionists. Standing on the solid ground of the Scripture, it scrutinizes the arguments of the revisionists and responds to them point-by-point. It critically examines and refutes the teachings of the most prominent proponents of pro-gay theology, including the Rev. Dr. Mel White and the Rev. Elder Don Eastman of the LGBTQ Religious Archives Network.

In reality, as this book will demonstrate, an honest reading of the Bible leads to the unequivocal conclusion that homosexual relations are prohibited by God and are characterized as sin. Seeking to correct the course of revisionist theologians, this book aims to set the Christian church back on the correct course of orthodox Christian doctrine in regards to the historic and consensual teachings of the Christian Church on gender, sex and marriage.

CHAPTER 2. THE HUMAN RIGHTS CAMPAIGN'S TEACHINGS ON HOMOSEXUALITY

The Human Rights Campaign, in its article, "What Does the Bible Say About Homosexuality?" written by Myles Markham,[1] argues that poor biblical scholarship is at the heart of the claim that homosexuality is forbidden by God. However, what quickly comes to light upon reading the article is that it is in fact the Human Rights Campaign's article, not the views of traditional Christianity, that is the result of poor, or shall we say absent, biblical scholarship. The Human Rights Campaign's article is riddled with erroneous assertions. When alleging a claim is supported by some biblical text, the author provides biblical verses that run directly contrary to rather than support the proposed assertions. Overall, the article's overall assertion that what is forbidden in the Bible is sexual violence, not committed, loving homosexual partnerships, is given no valid biblical support.

The article opens with a discussion of six passages that address homosexuality and proceeds to state:

> While the six passages that address same-sex eroticism in the ancient world are negative about the practices they mention, there is no evidence that these in any way speak to same-sex relationships of love and mutuality. To the contrary, the amount of cultural, historical and linguistic data surrounding how sexuality in the cultures of the biblical authors operated demonstrates that what was being condemned in the

---

[1] Myles Markham, "What Does the Bible Say About Homosexuality?" Human Rights Campaign Foundation, available at <https://www.hrc.org/resources/what-does-the-bible-say-about-homosexuality>.

Bible is very different than the committed same-sex partnerships we know and see today. The stories of Sodom and Gomorrah (Genesis 19) and the Levite's concubine (Judges 19) are about sexual violence and the Ancient Near East's stigma toward violating male honor. The injunction that "man must not lie with man" (Leviticus 18:22, 20:13) coheres with the context of a society anxious about their health, continuing family lineages, and retaining the distinctiveness of Israel as a nation. Each time the New Testament addresses the topic in a list of vices (1 Corinthians 6:9, 1 Timothy 1:10), the argument being made is more than likely about the sexual exploitation of young men by older men, a practice called pederasty, and what we read in the Apostle Paul's letter to the Romans is a part of a broader indictment against idolatry and excessive, self-centered lust that is driven by desire to "consume" rather than to love and to serve as outlined for Christian partnership elsewhere in the Bible. While it is likely that Jews and Christians in the 1st century had little to no awareness of a category like sexual orientation, this doesn't mean that the biblical authors were wrong. What it does mean, at a minimum, is that continued opposition toward same-sex relationships and LGBTQ+ identities must be based on something other than these biblical texts, which brings us back to a theology of Christian marriage or partnership.

There are multiple issues with these arguments, including:

- The article claims that the account is Judges is concerned with the ancient Near East's stigma toward violating male honor. The text offers no citation to support this assertion. In fact, the ancient Near East, like the ancient Near East, like the modern Near East, is far more concerned about violating female honor and preserving women's virginity than it is about male honor and virginity, to the point where in many Near East countries, honor killings are committed against women accused of fornication.
- The article claims that each time the New Testament addresses homosexuality in a list of vices (1 Corinthians 6:9, 1 Timothy 1:10), "the argument being made is more than likely about the sexual exploitation of young men by older men." This claim has no textual support whatsoever. 1 Corinthians 6:9 and 1 Timothy 1:10 clearly reference "men who have sex with men" and those "practicing homosexuality." There is not a single reference to young or old men in either of the texts.
- The article claims that "what we read in the Apostle Paul's letter to the Romans is a part of a broader indictment against idolatry and excessive, self-centered lust that is driven by desire to 'consume'

rather than to love and to serve as outlined for Christian partnership elsewhere in the Bible." This claim is directly contradicted by the very text it sets out to interpret. Romans 1:26-28 pronounces God's judgment on women who "exchanged natural sexual relations for unnatural ones" and men who "abandoned natural relations with women and were inflamed with lust for one another." These verses are followed by a litany of sins that have nothing to do with consumption, including "envy, murder, strife, deceit and malice" (Rom 1:29) and gossip, slander, hatred of God, insolence, arrogance, boasting and disobedience of parents (Rom 1:30).

The penultimate paragraph of the article goes on to emphasize the importance of love, empathy and compassion, regardless of gender, in the Christian walk. It states that Christian partnership "creates an opportunity to live out God's love. While some kind of difference seems to be important in embodying this metaphor, understanding that all our differences can lead to empathy, compassion, good listening, sacrifice, and what it means to 'love our neighbor as ourselves,' there is scant evidence that it is our biology or our views of gender that are the required difference." No orthodox Christian would disagree with this. Christians support love, and believe that men can and should love both men and women, and that women can and should love both men and women. A man or woman can love one woman or one man or more than one man or more than one woman. Ideally, all Christians would love all of humanity. It is not love that Christians oppose. Rather, it is the homosexual acts prohibited by the Scriptures that orthodox Christians oppose.

CHAPTER 3. HOMOSEXUALITY: NOT A SIN, NOT A SICKNESS?

A. OVERVIEW

Rev. Elder Don Eastman, in his article, "Homosexuality: Not a Sin, Not a Sickness Part II 'What The Bible Does and Does Not Say...'"[2] espouses the view that the Bible, when properly read, does not characterize homosexuality as a sin or a sickness. Rev. Eastman's article contains countless fallacies and mischaracterizations of scriptural teaching, the most serious of which are presented and refuted herein.

B. SODOM AND GOMORRAH'S SINS WERE NOT RELATED TO HOMOSEXUALITY

Rev. Eastman raises a series of points to suggest that the sin of Sodom and Gomorrah was not related to homosexuality. Each of his points is presented herein and refuted in turn.

1. Prior Judgment on the Cities

Rev. Eastman writes:

---

[2] Rev. Elder Don Eastman, "Homosexuality: Not a Sin, Not a Sickness Part II 'What The Bible Does and Does Not Say...'" Religious Institute (1990), available at <http://religiousinstitute.org/denom_statements/homosexuality-not-a-sin-not-a-sickness-part-ii-what-the-bible-does-and-does-not-say>.

First, the judgment on these cities for their wickedness had been announced prior to the alleged homosexual incident.

God's judgment of Sodom and Gomorrah in Genesis 18 was not linked to their attempted rape of Lot's guests in Genesis 19. God makes clear that his judgment related to Sodom and Gomorrah's past sin (the Lord said, "the outcry against Sodom and Gomorrah is so great and their sin so grievous that I will go down and see if what they have done is as bad as the outcry that has reached me" (Gen 18:20-21)). The attempted rape of Lot's guests in Genesis 19 was a manifestation of pervasive sin that had been endemic to Sodom; it was not the sin that prompted God's judgment of the city.

2. All of Sodom's People Participated in the Assault on Lot, Homosexuals Are a Small Minority

Rev. Eastman writes:

> Second, all of Sodom's people participated in the assault on Lot's house; in no culture has more than a small minority of the population been homosexual.

The Scripture does not state that all of Sodom's people participated in the assault on Lot's home. Rather, it states that "all the men from every part of the city of Sodom" (Gen 19:4) participated. In this way, the Scripture alludes to the homosexual nature of the attempted assault of Lot's guests.

Rev. Eastman makes a sweeping statement about the percentage of homosexuals in all cultures, presumably throughout time, but without offering any research, evidence or citations. In fact, the percentage of homosexuals in any country or culture is widely disputed. Regardless of this percentage, Rev. Eastman offers no evidence to counter the possibility that regardless of how many of Sodom's residents identified as homosexuals, some or all of them may have had some homosexual proclivities, at least enough to drive them to attempt to rape Lot's guests.

In addition, Rev. Eastman ignores the possibility that Genesis 19:4, in deploying the term "all the men from every part of the city," is employing hyperbole, which is commonly used throughout the Bible to illustrate a point. In John 4, for example, Jesus revealed to a Samaritan woman that she had five husbands and that the man she had was not her husband (John 4:17-18). The Samaritan woman then testified that Jesus "told me everything I ever did" (John 4:29). Of course, Jesus had not in that brief conversation told her *everything* that she ever did. The Samaritan woman used hyperbole to convey the incisive insight of the Messiah, whom she had just encountered. In the same way, Genesis 19 is not likely trying to convey that *every* man in Sodom had participated in the attempted rape of Lot's guests. It wouldn't be practical for every male resident to even fit on Lot's front step as the angry mob demanded Lot's visitors. Most likely, the Bible is employing hyperbole to convey the fact that a great multitude of Sodom's residents had gathered at Lot's home to demand that Lot turn over the guests for the men to know carnally.

3. Lot's Offer to Release His Daughters Suggests the Intruders were Heterosexuals

Rev. Eastman writes:

> Third, Lot's offer to release his daughters suggests he knew his neighbors to have heterosexual interests.

On this basis, Rev. Eastman suggests that the intruders could not have been homosexuals because Lot offered them his daughters, "who have never slept with a man" (Gen 19:8).

Here, Rev. Eastman's fallacy is to equate a person's sexual orientation to the type of sexual intercourse offered to them. Therefore, if a woman offers to have sex with a man, the man cannot be a homosexual. If Lot offered to have his daughters have sex with his intruders, the intruders could not be homosexuals.

The logic that Rev. Eastman employs is deeply flawed. If his reasoning is correct, one can conclude that if a person is offered a meat entrée, he cannot be a vegetarian. If a person's tastes and orientation are not based on inherent desires or inclinations, but rather on what they are offered, then there is no such thing as an inherent sexual orientation, since a person at any moment can be proffered sex with a man or a woman.

Ch. 3. Homosexuality: Not a Sin, Not a Sickness?

Finally, even if Rev. Eastman is correct both in that Lot's neighbors had heterosexual interests and that Lot knew this, this does not preclude the possibility that Lot's neighbors also had homosexual interests. It is clear that Sodom's residents had a sexual interest in Lot's guests. Otherwise, Lot would not have attempted to satiate their interests by offering up his daughters rather than his male guests ("Look, I have two daughters who have never slept with a man. Let me bring them out to you, and you can do what you like with them. But don't do anything to these men, for they have come under the protection of my roof" (Gen 19:8)).

4. If the Issue Were Sexual, God Would Not Have Spared Lot, Who Had Incest with His Daughters

a. Overview

Rev. Eastman writes:

> Fourth, if the issue was sexual, why did God spare Lot, who immediately commits incest with his daughters?

Here, Rev. Eastman betrays a fundamental understanding of both the Scripture and of sin. The Scripture does not state that Lot committed incest with his daughters. At no time did he voluntarily exercise free will. Rather, the Scripture makes clear that his daughters intoxicated him and Lot was not aware of when either daughter laid with him:

> Gen 19:32 Let's get our father to drink wine and then sleep with him and preserve our family line through our father."
>
> Gen 19:33 That night they got their father to drink wine, and the older daughter went in and slept with him. He was not aware of it when she lay down or when she got up.
>
> Gen 19:34 The next day the older daughter said to the younger, "Last night I slept with my father. Let's get him to drink wine again tonight, and you go in and sleep with him so we can preserve our family line through our father."
>
> Gen 19:35 So they got their father to drink wine that night also, and the younger daughter went in and slept with him. Again he was not aware of it when she lay down or when she got up.

b. Lot Did Not Sin; He Was a Righteous Man

Sin is comprised of an act of the free will. One cannot sin if he lacks capacity. A drunk cannot commit sin, just as a person who acts due to compulsion cannot commit sin. As Genesis 19 makes clear, Lot's daughters were morally responsible for committing incest with their father. They generated the idea and carried it out by first intoxicating their father. Lot was a victim of the crime who lacked awareness of the acts at the time they were committed.

Under modern criminal law, if a man has sexual intercourse with a woman while she is sleeping or after she is so intoxicated that she is unaware of the intercourse, the law concludes that the woman did not freely give her consent. Therefore, the intercourse was involuntary and the man is guilty of rape. The situation of Lot was no different. He was so intoxicated that he was unaware that his daughters laid with him. He did not give consent. Both the intoxication and the subsequent intercourse were the doing of his daughters, not of Lot. In fact, Lot is depicted by Peter as "a righteous man, who was distressed by the depraved conduct of the lawless" (2Pe 2:7).

c. Even if Lot Had Sinned, the Sin Would Have Been After His Rescue

Yet even if Lot had capacity and voluntarily committed incest with his daughters, the acts were committed after Lot was rescued from the destruction of Sodom and Gomorrah. God judges us for acts we have committed, not for future acts that we future acts that we might theoretically commit. Rev. Eastman is therefore wrong to suggest that God would not have rescued Lot if the sin of Sodom was sexual because Lot would later commit sexual sin. It is entirely possible for God to rescue a person but for that person to later turn against God and sin. Such people who are redeemed by God only to turn against God, are discussed throughout the Scripture. Peter writes of them as follows (2Pe 2:20-21):

> If they have escaped the corruption of the world by knowing our Lord and Savior Jesus Christ and are again entangled in it and are overcome, they are worse off at the end than they were at the beginning.
>
> It would have been better for them not to have known the way of righteousness, than to have known it and then to turn their backs on the sacred command that was passed on to them.

Ch. 3. Homosexuality: Not a Sin, Not a Sickness?

d. God Could Rescue a Sexual Sinner and Still Condemn Sodom and Gomorrah

Yet even if Lot engaged in sexual sin prior to the judgment of Sodom and Gomorrah, God still could have rescued Lot and condemned the cities. God is sovereign and saves whom He wills. "God has mercy on whom he wants to have mercy" (Rom 9:18). God used Joshua to rescue Rahab, a prostitute (Jos 6:25). If God would save a prostitute, surely he could save any person who had committed sexual sin.

e. Homosexuality Falls into a Special Class of Sin

Finally, even if Rev. Eastman were correct that God could not have judged Sodom and Gomorrah for sexual sin because He rescue Lot for sexual sin, we must recognize that homosexuality is a special class of sin that is repeatedly condemned in Scripture. While all sin has the potential to separate man from God, homosexuality, like adultery, is condemned as causing man to forfeit the kingdom of heaven (1Co 6:9-10):

> Neither the sexually immoral nor idolaters nor adulterers nor _men who have sex with men_ nor thieves nor the greedy nor drunkards nor slanderers nor swindlers will inherit the kingdom of God.

5. No Other Passages Refer to the Issue of Homosexuality

Finally, Rev. Eastman writes:

> Most importantly, why do all the other passages of Scripture referring to this account fail to raise the issue of homosexuality?

It is not necessary for the other passages of Scripture to explicitly raise the issue of homosexuality. That Lot's intruders wanted to have sex with Lot's guests is made very clear by the passage itself (Gen 19:5):

> NKJV: And they called to Lot and said to him, "Where are the men who came to you tonight? Bring them out to us that we may know them carnally."
>
> NIV: They called to Lot, "Where are the men who came to you tonight? Bring them out to us so that we can have sex with them."
>
> ISV: They called out to Lot and asked, "Where are the men who came to visit you tonight? Bring them out to us so we can have sex with them!"

KJV: And they called unto Lot, and said unto him, Where are the men which came in to thee this night? bring them out unto us, that we may know them.

Rev. Eastman's suggestion that the intruders came to Lot's home merely to identity Lot's guests rather than know them carnally has no scriptural or logical support whatsoever. If the intruders showed up simply to demand the identity cards of Lot's guests, Lot would not have replied to them to not "do this wicked thing" (Gen 19:7). The fact that Lot offered the intruders his "two daughters who have never slept with a man" to "do what you like with them," but to spare "these men, for they have come under the protection of my roof" (Gen 19:8) makes the intruders' intent to rape Lot's guests crystal clear. If the men were merely coming to identity Lot's guests, Lot would have had no incentive to dissuade them from their intended criminal behavior by offering them his virgin daughters.

6. The True Reason for Sodom and Gomorrah's Destruction

Rev. Eastman writes:

> Ezekiel 16:48-50 states it clearly. The people of Sodom, like many people today, had abundance of material goods. But they failed to meet the needs of the poor, and they worshipped idols. The sins of injustice and idolatry plague every generation. We stand under the same judgment if we create false gods or treat others with injustice.

The passage that Rev. Eastman quotes states as follows (Eze 16:48-50):

> As surely as I live, declares the Sovereign LORD, your sister Sodom and her daughters never did what you and your daughters have done. "Now this was the sin of your sister Sodom: She and her daughters were arrogant, overfed and unconcerned; they did not help the poor and needy. They were haughty and did detestable things before me. Therefore I did away with them as you have seen.

To be sure, Sodom had many sins. As Ezekiel pointed out, these sins included arrogance, gluttony (being overfed), a lack of concern for the poor and needy and haughtiness. However, there is nothing in the Book of Ezekiel that suggests that these were Sodom's exclusive sins. Rather,

Ezekiel points out to "detestable things" that Sodom committed. This is a catch all that very well could encompass Sodom's sexual sin, including homosexuality.

Moreover, the account of Genesis 19:15, where Sodom's residents intrude upon Lot's home to demand Lot's guests to have sexual relations with them, is clear biblical evidence of Sodom's sin of homosexuality.

7. Jude 1:7 Confirms that Sexual Immorality Was the Cause of Sodom and Gomorrah's Destruction

In addition to the aforementioned arguments based on Scripture and reason, Jude 1:7 lays to rest any further debate as to the true cause of the destruction of Sodom and Gomorrah:

> Jude 1:7 In a similar way, Sodom and Gomorrah and the surrounding towns gave themselves up to sexual immorality and perversion. They serve as an example of those who suffer the punishment of eternal fire.

It was sexual immorality, and, in particular, the attempted homosexual rape as described in Genesis 19, not a lack of hospitality, that was the cause of Sodom's destruction.

C. CHRISTIANS CANNOT JUDGE HOMOSEXUALITY BECAUSE THEY DO NOT FOLLOW THE OLD TESTAMENT LAW

Rev. Eastman argues that Christians cannot judge homosexuality because they do not follow the Old Testament law:

> Christians today do not follow the rules and rituals described in Leviticus. But some ignore its definitions of their own "uncleanness" while quoting Leviticus to condemn "homosexuals." Such abuse of Scripture distorts the Old Testament meaning and denies a New Testament message.

As discussed below, Rev. Eastman is mistaken on multiple fronts.

1. There Is a Difference between Violating God's Law and Repenting, on the One Hand, and Disregarding God's Law, on the Other

Rev. Eastman misunderstands the position of Christianity with respect to the Old Testament. Christians do not ignore the Old Testament Laws. They view the laws as God's model for holy living. However, Christians acknowledge that they cannot comply with the Law; they rely on God's mercy and grace for their salvation.

Yet this does not mean that Christians uphold violations of God's law. This is a fundamental difference between orthodox Christian doctrine and the views espoused by Rev. Eastman. Orthodox Christianity does not uphold, promote or characterize as an acceptable choice living in a way that contradicts God's law. While Christians recognize that "all have sinned and fall short of God's glory" (Rom 3:23) and that they are in need for God's salvation, Rev. Eastman fails to recognize homosexual acts as violations of God's law requiring repentance, mercy and forgiveness.

Therefore, it is not that Christians ignore the Levitical law and focus only on homosexuality. Rather, Christians recognize all of God's law as valid, for "not the smallest letter, not the least stroke of a pen, will by any means disappear from the Law until everything is accomplished" (Mat 5:18). The law was fulfilled by Christ's sacrifice at Calvary, but this does not mean that the law is irrelevant. It means that we have an open door to redemption through falling at the feet of Christ in repentance for our violations of the law. Yet this door closes when our hearts are hardened and we refuse to recognize our sin. Our hearts are hardened when we refuse to recognize sin as sin and instead uphold it as acceptable behavior or even promote it. This is the fundamental difference between a Christian who has violated the Old Testament law through, for example, greed, gluttony, adultery and fornication, and yet has turned away from his sin through repentance and asking for forgiveness, and the person who engages in homosexual acts with complete disregard for God's prohibition of such acts.

2. Homosexuality Is Not Only Prohibited in the Levitical Law; the New Testament Also Prohibits It

The second error that Rev. Eastman makes is his failure to acknowledge that homosexuality is prohibited not only in the Levitical law, but also, in the New Testament:

Rom 1:26-28 Because of this, God gave them over to shameful lusts. Even *their women exchanged natural sexual relations for unnatural ones*. In the same way the men also abandoned natural relations with women and were inflamed with lust for one another. *Men committed shameful acts with other men*, and received in themselves the due penalty for their error. Furthermore, just as they did not think it worthwhile to retain the knowledge of God, so God gave them over to a depraved mind, so that they do what ought not to be done.

1Co 6:9-10 Or do you not know that wrongdoers will not inherit the kingdom of God? Do not be deceived: Neither the sexually immoral nor idolaters nor adulterers nor *men who have sex with men* nor thieves nor the greedy nor drunkards nor slanderers nor swindlers will inherit the kingdom of God.

1Ti 1:9-11 We also know that the law is made not for the righteous but for lawbreakers and rebels, the ungodly and sinful, the unholy and irreligious, for those who kill their fathers or mothers, for murderers, for the sexually immoral, for those *practicing homosexuality*, for slave traders and liars and perjurers—and for whatever else is contrary to the sound doctrine that conforms to the gospel concerning the glory of the blessed God, which he entrusted to me.

This fact makes it unnecessary to rely on the story of Sodom and Gomorrah and the Levitical law to point to the Bible's prohibition of homosexuality.

D. LEVITICUS WAS INTENDED TO PROHIBIT "IDOLATRY"; THE REFERENCE TO HOMOSEXUALITY IS DUE TO MISTRANSLATION

Rev. Eastman writes:

An abomination is that which God found detestable because it was unclean, disloyal, or unjust. Several Hebrew words were so translated, and the one found in Leviticus, *toevah*, is usually associated with idolatry, as in Ezekiel, where it occurs numerous times. Given the strong association of *toevah* with idolatry and the canaanite religious practice of cult prostitution, the use of *toevah* regarding male same-sex acts in Leviticus calls into question any conclusion that such condemnation also applies to loving, responsible homosexual relationships.

In effect, Dr. Eastman is arguing that if the reader examines Leviticus closely in the original Hebrew and with a view to the context of the rest of scripture, including Ezekiel, he will come to conclude that it is unlikely that the Bible prohibits homosexuality; rather, it prohibits idolatry. Rev. Eastman's argument is flawed on multiple levels, as discussed below.

1. Leviticus Prohibits Homosexuality whether To'evah Is Translated as "Abomination" or "Idolatry"

Even if we accept Rev. Eastman's argument with respect to the true meaning of the term "to'evah," his conclusion is fallacious. In fact, if to'evah means "idolatry" rather than "abomination," then the Levitical prohibition on homosexuality is even more pronounced. Equating a sin with idolatry is a condemnation in stronger terms than equating it with mere abomination. Of all the forms of sin in the Bible, idolatry finds itself at the pinnacle. In fact, the first of the two of the Ten Commandments revolve around the idea of idolatry. The first prohibits putting any god before God; the second prohibits making, bowing down before and worshiping idols.

In the New Testament, in the Council of Jerusalem, the apostle Peter declared that the Old Testament law has been fulfilled, but Christians were required to comply with four basic, timeless moral laws. Christians were to abstain from (Acts 15:29):

- things offered to idols;
- blood;
- things strangled; and
- sexual immorality.

The prohibition of acts associated with idolatry continued into the new covenant, highlighting the gravity of the sin of idolatry.

Therefore, even if we accept Rev. Eastman's argument at face value, the prohibition on homosexuality in Leviticus would be no less pronounced.

2. The Prohibition on Homosexuality in Leviticus Is Clear Regardless of the Translation of "*To'evah*"

Regardless of how the term *to'evah* is translated, Leviticus's prohibition on homosexuality is crystal clear. It states, "You shall not lie with a male as with a woman" (Lev 18:22). Whether this is followed by "it is an abomination" or "it is idolatry" does not alter this prohibition.

3. The Verses Surrounding Leviticus 18:22 Place the Prohibition of Homosexuality within the Context of Sexual Sin, Including Incest, Adultery and Bestiality

The verses surrounding the prohibition on homosexuality found in Leviticus 18:22 list prohibited behaviors that are characterized as perversion, wickedness and abomination:

> Lev 18:6 "'No one is to approach *any close relative* to have sexual relations. I am the LORD.
>
> Lev 18:7 "'Do not dishonor your father by having *sexual relations with your mother* ...
>
> Lev 18:9 "'Do not have *sexual relations with your sister* ...
>
> Lev 18:20 "'Do not have *sexual relations with your neighbor's wife* and defile yourself with her ...
>
> Lev 18:22 "'Do not have *sexual relations with a man as one does with a woman*; that is detestable.
>
> Lev 18:23 "'Do not have *sexual relations with an animal* and defile yourself with it. A woman must not present herself to an animal to have sexual relations with it; that is a perversion.
>
> Lev 18:24 "'Do not defile yourselves in any of these ways, because this is how the nations that I am going to drive out before you became defiled ...

Whether we alter the term "abomination" found in Leviticus 18:22 to instead state "idolatry" does not alter God's clear commandment to refrain from these behaviors, which constitute sexual sin. In fact, if we remove the clause referring to abomination in Leviticus 18:22 altogether, the prohibition on homosexuality is not altered. It states, "Do not have sexual relations with a man as one does with a woman." It is difficult to argue that this is anything other than a prohibition.

Reading Leviticus 18:22 within the context of the versions that precede and follow it demonstrates that the prohibition of homosexuality found in Leviticus 18:22 is placed squarely amidst prohibitions of other forms of sexual sin: incest, adultery and bestiality.

E. CHRISTIANS ARE NO LONGER BOUND BY BIBLICAL LAW

Rev. Eastman writes:

> Rituals and Rules found in the Old Testament were given to preserve the distinctive characteristics of the religion and culture of Israel. But, as stated in Galatians 3:22-25, Christians are no longer bound by these Jewish laws. By faith we live in Jesus Christ, not in Leviticus. To be sure, ethical concerns apply to all cultures and peoples in every age. Such concerns were ultimately reflected by Jesus Christ, who said nothing about homosexuality, but a great deal about love, justice, mercy and faith.

Rev. Eastman is mistaken on two fronts:

1. The Israelites' Standing Out from Other Cultures was a Consequence, not the Purpose, of God's Law

First, rituals and rules found in the Old Testament were not given to preserve the distinctive characteristics of the religion and culture of Israel, as Rev. Eastman suggests. Rather, the "rules," or law, was given to Israel to point to God's standard of absolute holiness and to convict Israel of her sin, for "through the law we become conscious of our sin" (Rom 3:20). The law was given to direct God's people as to how to live in a way that honored God and love their neighbors. The fact that the Israelites, by following God's law, would distinguish themselves from the peoples around them was a consequence, not the purpose, of God's law.

2. Christians are not Free from the Old Testament Law; They Are Still Bound by the Spirit of the Law

Second, Rev. Eastman mischaracterizes Christians' freedom from the Levitical law. Citing Galatians 3:22-25, he states that Christians are no longer bound by Jewish laws. He also mischaracterizes what Jesus said about the law. Rev. Eastman writes that Jesus "said nothing about homosexuality."

In fact, Jesus said (Mat 5:17-19):

> Do not think that I have come to abolish the Law or the Prophets; I have not come to abolish them but to fulfill them. For truly I tell you, until heaven and earth disappear, not the smallest letter, not the least stroke of

a pen, will by any means disappear from the Law until everything is accomplished. Therefore anyone who sets aside one of the least of these commands and teaches others accordingly will be called least in the kingdom of heaven, but whoever practices and teaches these commands will be called great in the kingdom of heaven.

While Jesus fulfilled the Old Testament law through His perfect living and self-sacrifice, its moral principles continue to apply. This is why Peter, at the Council of Jerusalem, held that Christians were to comply with four basic, timeless, moral laws. Christians were to abstain from (Acts 15:29):

- things offered to idols;
- blood;
- things strangled; and
- sexual immorality.

This remnant of the Old Testament law demonstrates that moral principles relating to idolatry and sexual purity continue to apply.

Today, Christians are to keep the moral law, but not as a means of earning salvation. Their salvation was already sealed through the blood of Jesus. Rather, Christians should keep the moral law out of their deep and abiding love for God. Loving God means loving what God loves, including justice and mercy, and therefore, keeping the moral law.

3. It Is Unknown Whether Jesus Said Anything About Homosexuality

Rev. Eastman writes that Jesus "said nothing about homosexuality, but a great deal about love, justice, mercy and faith." Neither Rev. Eastman nor any other person other than Jesus himself knows what Jesus may have said about homosexuality. Jesus lived on the earth 33 years and we have no record of every word that He ever stated. The Gospels are an abbreviated summary of His life and teachings, and they are in no way intended as a life transcript of every word Jesus uttered. Therefore, Rev. Eastman cannot claim that Jesus "said nothing about homosexuality."

Yet even if Jesus never uttered a word about homosexuality, the New Testament is replete with other prohibitions of homosexuality, including in Romans 1:26-28, 1 Corinthians 6:9-10 and 1 Timothy 1:9-11 (homosexuality is "contrary to the sound doctrine that conforms to the gospel concerning the glory of the blessed God").

F. ROMANS 1:26-28 DOES NOT CONDEMN HOMOSEXUALITY BETWEEN LOVING, COMMITTED PARTNERS

Rev. Eastman argues that of the New Testament verses that discuss homosexuality, Romans 1:26-28 presents homosexuality in the harshest terms. However, when put in its proper context, Romans 1:26-28 does not actually condemn homosexuality between loving, committed partners. Rather, it only condemns homosexuality performed as part of pagan idolatrous rituals and the Isis cult in Rome. Rev. Eastman writes:

> The book of Romans was written to Jewish and Gentile Christians in Rome, who would have been familiar with the infamous sexual excesses of their contemporaries, especially Roman emperors. They would also have been aware of tensions in the early Church regarding Gentiles and observance of the Jewish laws, as noted in Acts 15 and Paul's letter to the Galatians. Jewish laws in Leviticus mentioned male same-sex acts _in the context of idolatry_.
>
> The _homosexual practices cited in Romans 1:24-27 were believed to result from idolatry_ and are associated with some very serious offenses as noted in Romans 1. Taken in this larger context, it should be obvious that such acts are significantly different from loving, responsible lesbian and gay relationships seen today.

Rev. Eastman's argument is flawed on multiple levels. First, it ignores the plain text of Romans. Nowhere does Paul suggest that homosexual relations between "loving, committed partners" fell into an exception to the prohibition on homosexuality. Rather, Paul paints a blanket statement condemning homosexual relations. He writes:

> Rom 1:26 God gave them over to shameful lusts. Even their women exchanged natural sexual relations for unnatural ones.
>
> Rom 1:27 In the same way the men also abandoned natural relations with women and were inflamed with lust for one another. Men committed shameful acts with other men, and received in themselves the due penalty for their error.

Women having sex with one another is characterized within the context of "shameful lusts"; men having sex with one another is characterized as "shameful acts." If such relations were perfectly acceptable to Paul unless they were performed as part of pagan worship, then Paul would have made this clear. He would have written that "God gave women over to shameful lusts, exchanging natural sexual relations for unnatural ones without any long-term commitment and outside of monogamous marriage; men abandoned natural relations with women and were inflamed with lust for one another, exchanging natural sexual relations for unnatural ones without any long-term commitment and outside of monogamous marriage." Of course, Paul says no such thing. He condemned all sexual relations as "shameful" and contrary to God's will.

The second problem with Rev. Eastman's argument is it ignores 2,000 years of church history. The Christian church, prior to the revisionist doctrines of certain splinter groups in the last two to three decades, has always understood homosexuality in general—not merely homosexual acts performed within the context of pagan rituals—to be sin. The Orthodox Church, which boasts nearly 2,000 years of an unbroken lineage tracing back to Jesus Christ and the Twelve Apostles, unequivocally condemns homosexuality as sin. The Assembly of Canonical Orthodox Bishops of the United States, for example, states that "[l]ike adultery and fornication, homosexual acts are condemned by Scripture." It would be difficult for a new splinter Christian group founded in the last few years to claim to have more authority to interpret what Paul meant when he condemned homosexuality than the Orthodox Church, which has had an unbroken lineage that traces back to Paul. If indeed Paul meant that only homosexual acts performed pursuant to idolatrous rituals was forbidden, then how is it that the first century church missed this? How is it that the second century missed it? How is it that the church fathers, for nearly 2,000 years, understood Paul to condemn homosexuality as a sin? How is it that over 2,000 years of church history, all of the church fathers, apostles, popes and patriarchs missed Paul's message, until Rev. Eastman and other revisionists that emerged in the past few decades came to understand Paul's hidden message? And why did Paul hide his message so well rather than promulgate it clearly for the entire world to understand?

Third, if Paul were only referring to homosexual relations "believed to result from idolatry," as Rev. Eastman suggests, then there would be no need to even mention homosexuality. Paul makes the prohibition on idolatry in Romans 1 very clear. Similarly, God prohibits only homosexuality within the context of idolatry, then there would be no need to list homosexuality as a separate offense from idolatry in the lists of sins given throughout the Old and New Testaments. For example, in 1 Corinthians 6:9, Paul lists both idolaters and "men who have sex with men" (NIV) or "homosexuals" (NKJV) among those who will not inherit the Kingdom of God. If only men who engage in homosexuality as a part of pagan cult worship were excluded, then there would be no need to mention them, because Paul has already listed idolaters.

Indeed, the black letter of Paul's letters, the historic position of the Christian church and the overall scriptural context confirm that homosexuality is sin, and there is little that Rev. Eastman offers to overcome or change this view.

G. ROMANS 1:26 DOES NOT CONDEMN LESBIANISM; IT CONDEMNS WOMEN WHO PLAY A DOMINANT ROLE IN HETEROSEXUAL RELATIONSHIPS

Rev. Eastman writes:

> Romans 1:26 is the only statement in the Bible with a possible reference to lesbian behavior, although the specific intent of this verse is unclear. Some authors have seen in this passage a reference to women adopting a dominant role in heterosexual relationships. Given the repressive cultural expectations placed on women in Paul's time, such a meaning may be possible.

Rev. Eastman's claim is flawed on multiple levels. First, it ignores the plain text of Romans 1:26, which makes clear that it is referring to sexual relations, not to social relations between a man and a woman in a heterosexual relationship. Romans 1:26 very specifically references "shameful lusts." These shameful lusts are the lusts of women to have sex with one another, not the adoption by women of dominant roles in heterosexual relationships. Romans 1:26 also references the exchange of "natural sexual relations for unnatural ones." Again, the relation of the verse to sexual relations is unequivocal.

Rev. Eastman's second error is to suggest that if a woman plays a dominant role in a heterosexual relationship (i.e., she takes the decisions in a heterosexual marriage), that this is sin. It is quite ironic that Rev. Eastman, who adopts a liberal, progressive revisionist interpretation of scripture to make room for homosexuality would do so at the expense of women empowerment. His strained interpretation of scripture that is intended to make room for lesbianism at the same time condemns empowered women and curbs female advancement.

H. "Homosexuals" in 1 Corinthians 6:9 Is a Mistranslation

Next, Rev. Eastman argues that "homosexuals" in 1 Corinthians 6:9 is a mistranslation.

> In I Corinthians 6:9, Paul condemns those who are "effeminate" and "abusers of themselves with mankind," as translated in the King James version. Unfortunately, some new translations are worse, rendering these words "homosexuals." Recent scholarship unmasks the homophobia behind such mistranslations.

Following is a sampling of translations of 1 Corinthians 6:9-10:

KJV	NKJV	NIV
9 Be not deceived:	9 Do not be deceived.	9 Do not be deceived:
neither _fornicators_,	Neither _fornicators_,	Neither the _sexually immoral_
nor idolaters,	nor idolaters,	nor idolaters
nor adulterers,	nor adulterers,	nor adulterers
nor _effeminate_,	nor _homosexuals_,	_nor men who have sex with men_
nor _abusers of themselves with mankind_,	nor _sodomites_,	

10 Nor thieves, nor covetous, nor drunkards, nor revilers, nor extortioners, shall inherit the kingdom of God.	10 nor thieves, nor covetous, nor drunkards, nor revilers, nor extortioners will inherit the kingdom of God.	10 nor thieves nor the greedy nor drunkards nor slanderers nor swindlers will inherit the kingdom of God.

Rev. Eastman's argument is flawed on multiple levels. First, even if he were correct modern translations of the Bible mistranslate the original Greek term μαλακός / *malakos* (G3120) as homosexual rather than as effeminate, the following term, ἀρσενοκοίτης / *arsenokotēs* (G733), which refers to one who lies with a male as with a female (*i.e.*, a sodomite or homosexual) makes the prohibition on homosexuality clear.

Second, even if neither μαλακός / *malakos* (G3120) nor ἀρσενοκοίτης / *arsenokotēs* (G733) referred to homosexuality, the rest of the verse makes the prohibition on homosexuality clear. Paul prohibits fornication and adultery. Active homosexuals necessarily commit fornication because Christianity only recognizes marriage between a man and a woman. Therefore, any sexual relations between two men or two women is necessarily outside of marriage and thus constitutes fornication. Moreover, such sexual relations may constitute adultery, which Paul also prohibits, if at least one of the partners to the homosexual acts is married.

I. THERE IS "NO LAW AGAINST LOVE"

Rev. Eastman's next argument is that homosexual relations between two loving, committed same-sex partners cannot be against scripture because there is "no law against love." Rev. Eastman writes:

> The rarity with which Paul discusses any form of same-sex behavior and the ambiguity in references attributed to him make it extremely unsound to conclude any sure position in the New Testament on homosexuality, especially in the context of loving, responsible relationships. Since any arguments must be made from silence, it is much more reliable to turn to great principles of the Gospel taught by Jesus Christ and the Apostles. Love God with all your heart, and love your neighbor as yourself. Do not

judge others, lest you be judged. The fruit of the Holy Spirit is love ... against such there is no law.

There are multiple problems with Rev. Eastman's argument. Just because there is no law against love does not make it acceptable to have sexual relations with whomever and whatever one desires. A person might love his mother, but this does not make sexual relations with her proper. A person might love his dog, but this does not make sexual relations with it proper. A person might love his neighbor's wife, but this does not make sexual relationship with her proper. In the same way, a man might love another man, but this does not make sexual relations with him proper.

While Rev. Eastman is correct that love is at the very center of Christian teaching, love does not create blanket tolerance for any form of sexual conduct that one wishes. God has given very strict guidelines on human sexuality. He has banned all forms of sexual relations outside of those between a man and a woman in a committed marriage. In Leviticus, incest, homosexuality, bestiality and adultery are all prohibited. In the New Testament, the injunction to maintain sexual purity is restated in Acts 15:20. Prohibitions on homosexuality are restated in Romans, 1 Corinthians and 1 Timothy.

Rev. Eastman argues that it is "extremely unsound to conclude any sure position in the New Testament on homosexuality, especially in the context of loving, responsible relationships." It is ironic that Rev. Eastman makes this argument because he, in fact, articulates a sure position on homosexuality—i.e., the Bible does not condemn homosexuality within the context of loving, committed relationships. Of course, this runs contrary to clear injunctions against homosexuality found in both the Old and New Testaments, in addition to being contrary to 2,000 years of church teaching.

J. Insights from Other Bible Scholars

Rev. Eastman concludes his piece with a series of quotes from Bible scholars who argue that there is no prohibition of homosexuality in the

Bible. We will examine each of the quotes, which are revisionist and problematic in multiple respects.

1. Robin Scroggs, Professor of Biblical Theology, Union Theological Seminary, New York City

Rev. Eastman quotes Professor Robin Scroggs, who writes:

> "The homosexuality the New Testament opposes is the pederasty of the Greco-Roman culture; the attitudes toward pederasty and, in part, the language used to oppose it are informed by the Jewish background."
>
> Robin Scroggs, Professor of Biblical Theology, Union Theological Seminary, New York City

Professor Scroggs is mistaken. The Bible makes not a single reference to the pederasty of the Greco-Roman culture or to pederasty in general. Pederasty in the Bible can only be deemed to be prohibited inasmuch as pederasty is a form of homosexuality, which is clearly prohibited in Genesis, the Levitical law, the book of Judges and throughout the New Testament. To argue that the references to homosexuality throughout the Old and New Testaments are intended to apply narrowly only to sexual relations between a man and a boy is to add to the Scriptures, a clear violation of the commands of the Scriptures ("I testify to everyone who hears the words of the prophecy of this book: if anyone adds to them, God will add to him the plagues which are written in this book" (Rev 22:18-19); "Do not add to what I command you and do not subtract from it, but keep the commands of the LORD your God that I give you" (Deu 4:2)).

If God were only concerned with sexual relations between men and boys, then He would have clearly banned pederasty in the Bible. But God is concerned with more than just sex between men and boys. He is concerned with all forms of sexuality that depart from how sexuality was designed—between a man and a woman for procreation within the context of marriage. Therefore, he prohibits incest (Lev 18:6), adultery (Lev 18:20) and bestiality (Lev 18:23).

Professor Scroggs' interpretation of the Bible is further debunked by Romans 1:26: "Because of this, God gave them over to shameful lusts. Even their women exchanged natural sexual relations for unnatural ones."

This verse proves that it is not only sexual relations between men and boys that constitute "shameful lusts" prohibited by God, but also, sexual relations between lesbian women as well. In this same manner, Romans 1:27 confirms that God is also concerned not only with sexual relations between men and boys, but also with sexual relations between homosexual men: "In the same way the men also abandoned natural relations with women and were inflamed with lust for one another. Men committed shameful acts with other men, and received in themselves the due penalty for their error."

2. Victor Paul Furnish, Professor of New Testament, Perkins School of Theology, Dallas

Rev. Eastman quotes Professor Victor Furnish, who writes:

> "One cannot be absolutely certain that the two key words in I Corinthians 6:9 are meant as references to male homosexual behavior."
>
> Victor Paul Furnish, Professor of New Testament, Perkins School of Theology, Dallas

Professor Furnish might be correct, but one does not need certainty with respect to the meaning of 1 Corinthians 6:9 to conclude that the Bible prohibits homosexuality. Regardless of whether the original Greek terms "μαλακός / *malakos*" (G3120) ("effeminate") and "ἀρσενοκοίτης / arsenokoitēs" (G733) ("lying with a male as with a female / sodomy") refer to homosexuality, the rest of 1 Corinthians 6:9 makes the prohibition on homosexuality clear. Paul prohibits fornication, which homosexual acts are necessarily a form of. Moreover, while there is some ambiguity in the term "μαλακός / *malakos*" (G3120) ("effeminate"), it is difficult to argue that the term ἀρσενοκοίτης / arsenokoitēs" (G733) ("lying with a male as with a female / sodomy") refers to anything other than homosexuality.

3. John J. McNeill, Adjunct Professor of Psychology, Union Theological Seminary, New York City

Rev. Eastman quotes Professor John McNeill, who writes:

> "The strongest New Testament argument against homosexual activity [as] intrinsically immoral has been derived traditionally from Romans

1:26, where this activity is indicated as *para physin*. The normal English translation for this has been 'against nature.' Two interpretations can be justified concerning what Paul meant by the phrase. It could refer to the individual pagan, who goes beyond his own sexual appetites in order to indulge in new sexual pleasure. The second possibility is that *physis* refers to the 'nature' of the chosen people who were forbidden by Levitical law to have homosexual relations."

John J. McNeill, Adjunct Professor of Psychology, Union Theological Seminary, New York City

Professor McNeil ignores the most obvious interpretation of Romans 1:26, which states that "God gave them over to shameful lusts. Even their women exchanged natural sexual relations for unnatural ones." By "natural relations," Paul is referring to sexual relations between men and women, which is how God intended human sexuality to be. "Unnatural relations" refer to sexual relations between women, which are contrary to nature. Paul is clearly pointing to homosexuality, as confirmed by Romans 1:27, which states that "the men *also* abandoned natural relations with women and were inflamed with lust for one another." Paul is juxtaposing natural relations (*i.e.*, heterosexual relations) with unnatural relations (*i.e.*, homosexual relations). Paul continues: "Men committed shameful acts with other men" (Rom 1:27). The shameful acts that men committed were not acts of theft or murder or bearing false witness. The acts were obviously sexual, because the men were "inflamed with lust for one another" (Rom 1:27).

Professor McNeill's proposed interpretations are based on scriptural additions that are found nowhere in the original text. Paul makes no reference to either pagans or to God's "chosen people" in Romans 1:26. In fact, based on the context of the surrounding verses, Paul is referring to humankind's sin in general, without restriction to either the pagans nor to God's chosen people. Paul refers to "all the godlessness and wickedness of people, who suppress the truth by their wickedness" (Rom 1:18) and who "exchanged the glory of the immortal God for images made to look like a mortal human being and birds and animals and reptiles" (Rom 1:23) and were turned over "to the sinful desires of their hearts to sexual impurity for the degrading of their bodies with one another" (Rom 1:24).

The second interpretation that Professor McNeill proffers is also problematic because there is nothing in the surrounding verses that suggests that Paul is referring only to the "chosen people." Paul is speaking about humanity's sin on a universal level. It would be unusual and counterintuitive that Paul would limit his discourse to the Jews. After all, his letter was to a Roman Gentile audience. Paul writes, "[t]o all in Rome who are loved by God and called to be his holy people: Grace and peace to you from God our Father and from the Lord Jesus Christ" (Rom 1:7) and "I do not want you to be unaware ... that I planned many times to come to you ... in order that I might have a harvest among you, just as I have had among the other Gentiles" (Rom 1:13).

4. William Countryman, Professor of New Testament, Church Divinity School of Pacific, Berkeley

Rev. Eastman quotes Professor William Countryman, who writes:

> "A close reading of Paul's discussion of homosexual acts in Romans 1 does not support the common modern interpretation of the passage. Paul did not deny the existence of a distinction between clean and unclean and even assumed that Jewish Christians would continue to observe the purity code. He refrained, however, from identifying physical impurity with sin or demanding that Gentiles adhere to that code."

> William Countryman, Professor of New Testament, Church Divinity School of Pacific, Berkeley

Professor Countryman appears to be confusing multiple concepts. The Jewish law maintained a distinction between clean and unclean foods. Christ abrogated that distinction:

> Mark 7:18 "Are you so dull?" he asked. "Don't you see that nothing that enters a person from the outside can defile them?
>
> Mark 7:19 For it doesn't go into their heart but into their stomach, and then out of the body." (In saying this, Jesus declared all foods clean.)
>
> Mark 7:20 He went on: "What comes out of a person is what defiles them.

God revealed this abrogation to Peter in a vision:

> Acts 10:13 Then a voice told him, "Get up, Peter. Kill and eat."

> Acts 10:14 "Surely not, Lord!" Peter replied. "I have never eaten anything impure or unclean."
>
> Acts 10:15 The voice spoke to him a second time, "Do not call anything impure that God has made clean."

It is thus not relevant whether Paul explicitly denied the distinction between clean and unclean foods. As a follower of Christ, Paul would have recognized that Christ made all food clean by fulfilling the Old Testament law.

A separate issue is that of sexual immorality. The fact that Christ made all food clean does not mean that all sexual acts suddenly became acceptable. In fact, throughout the New Testament, Christ and the apostles continued to denounce sexual immorality. Even Christ, after he declared all foods clean, went on to characterized "sexual immorality" as among the sins that make a person unclean:

> Mark 7:21 For it is from within, out of a person's heart, that evil thoughts come—sexual immorality, theft, murder,
>
> Mark 7:22 adultery, greed, malice, deceit, lewdness, envy, slander, arrogance and folly.
>
> Mark 7:23 All these evils come from inside and defile a person."

Paul maintained this distinction between clean and unclean sexual acts throughout his Epistles, including in Romans 1:26-28, 1 Corinthians 6:9-10 and 1 Timothy 1:9-11.

5. John Boswell, Professor of History, Yale University, New Haven

Rev. Eastman quotes Professor John Boswell, who writes:

> "The Hebrew word '*toevah*,' here translated 'abomination,' does not usually signify something intrinsically evil, like rape or theft (discussed elsewhere in Leviticus), but something which is <u>ritually unclean for Jews</u>, like eating pork or engaging in intercourse during menstruation, both of which are prohibited in these same chapters."
>
> John Boswell, Professor of History, Yale University, New Haven

Rev. Eastman does not give the full background or context of Professor Boswell's comment, but presumably, Professor Boswell is referring to the instance of *to'evah* found in Leviticus 18:22 (NKJV):

> Lev 18:22 You shall not lie with a male as with a woman. It is an abomination.

It is ironic that Rev. Eastman quotes Professor Boswell because Professor Boswell's argument does not fully align with the position proposed by Rev. Eastman in an earlier section of his essay, in which he states:

> An abomination is that which God found detestable because it was unclean, disloyal, or unjust. Several Hebrew words were so translated, and the one found in Leviticus, toevah, is usually associated *idolatry*, as in Ezekiel, where it occurs numerous times.

One could arguably reconcile the two positions by suggesting that idolatry is ritually unclean, and what is prohibited are certain acts only if they are ritually unclean.

However, this argument does not help Rev. Eastman. Whether homosexual relations are prohibited because they are an abomination or because they are ritually unclean, the book of Leviticus clearly prohibits them. Moreover, every one of the 118 instances of the term *to'evah* in the Old Testament is placed within a negative context that condemns the underlying behavior. For example, Leviticus 18:29 states (NKJV):

> For whoever commits any of these abominations, the persons who commit them shall be cut off from among their people.

Moreover, Professor Boswell's proposed translation of *to'evah* is problematic. Translating it as "ritually unclean" makes little sense in light of its use throughout the book of Proverbs, which uses it in a way to cast moral judgment in a way that cannot be bound to ritual. For example, Proverbs 15:26 states that the "thoughts of the wicked are an abomination to the LORD." Obviously, thoughts can be abominable, but they are not ritually unclean in the sense of the Old Testament law.

Presumably, Professor Boswell argues that *to'evah* refers to ritual uncleanliness in order to suggest that the Levitical prohibition on homosexuality does not apply to Christians. Employing this flawed translation to make this point is unnecessary because Christians already concede that they are not bound by the Levitical law. However, they are bound by prohibitions on sexual immorality found in the New Testament, which specifically repeats the Old Testament injunctions against homosexuality in Romans, 1 Corinthians and 1 Timothy, demonstrating that such relations continue to be off limits for Christians even in the New Testament covenant of grace.

CHAPTER 4. DOES THE SCRIPTURE AFFIRM THE LGBTQ COMMUNITY?

St. Hugh of Lincoln Episcopal Church of Elgin, Illinois published an article entitled "What Does the Bible Say about Homosexuality, Same-Sex Attraction, & Being Transgender?"[3] The article is riddled with errors, misconceptions and misinterpretations of scripture, which we respond to and refute herein.

A. GOD LOVES LGBTQ PEOPLE

Citing Romans 8:38 ("Nothing can separate us from the love of God"), St. Hugh of Lincoln Church (hereinafter, "St. Hugh Church" or "SHC") argues that God loves all people, including LGBTQs, and therefore, Christians should embrace rather than reject homosexuality, bisexuality and transgenderism as sin.

St. Hugh Church's first mistake is to equate identity with behavior. However, the two are distinct. An idolator is distinct from the act of idolatry. An adulterer is distinct from the act of adultery. A thief is distinct from the act of theft. A drunkard is distinct from the act of drinking. A slanderer is distinct from the act of the act of slander. In this same way, a homosexual is distinct from homosexual acts.

---

[3] St. Hugh of Lincoln Episcopal Church, "What Does the Bible Say about Homosexuality, Same-Sex Attraction, & Being Transgender?" (1 Mar. 2022), available at <https://www.sthugh.net/lgbtq-affirming-scripture>.

When Paul writes that nothing can separate us from the love of God (Rom 8:38), he is referring to God's infinite love of people, not of sin. Yet God's love does not extend to sinful acts. God does not love idolatry. He does not love adultery, nor does he love theft or drunkenness or homosexual acts.

By suggesting that because God loves all people, He embraces their sins is a misleading fallacy. Nothing in Scripture suggests that God approves of homosexual and bisexual acts and the changing of one's gender. To extend this logic beyond homosexuality would lead to the conclusion that because God loves all people, including idolaters, murderers, thieves and adulterers, God embraces idolatry, murder, theft and adultery.

B. GOD DID NOT MAKE A MISTAKE IN CREATING LGBTQ PEOPLE

St. Hugh Church goes on to argue that God made no mistake in creating LGBTQ people. Quoting Psalm 139:113-14 ("For you created my inmost being; you knit me together in my mother's womb. I praise you because I am fearfully and wonderfully made; your works are wonderful, I know that full well"), it argues that "[s]exual identity and gender identity are components of a person's personality, and as such are part of who God made each of us to be."

Yet if God created our inmost being and perfectly knit us together in the womb without any mistake, is it possible that he could have accidentally given a man a vagina, or a woman a penis? Is this not a mistake that the concerned individual must correct by changing his gender? It is ironic that SHC, on the one hand, affirms God's perfect craftmanship, and on the other hand, affirms a group that seeks to change their natural, God-given gender. If God makes no mistake, shouldn't a person born with the genetic makeup of a man embrace his male gender, in the same way that a woman born with the genetic makeup of a woman should embrace her female gender?

C. BEING LGBTQ IS NOT A SIN, BUT IF IT WERE, IT WOULD BE FORGIVEN

Citing 2 Corinthians 5:19, SHC argues as follows:

> All people are justified through Christ, including LGBTQ people ... This is not to say that being LGBTQ is a sin, but if it were, it would certainly be forgiven."

There are multiple issues with this statement. First, there is a difference between an inclination or an orientation, on the one hand, and conduct, on the other. Of course, merely having homosexual or bisexual inclinations, in and of itself, is not sin. A person is at liberty to either dismiss or act upon a temptation. It is not the act of being tempted that is the sin. After all, Christ, who remained sinless, suffered temptation in the desert after fasting for 40 days and 40 nights. However, Christ never gave in to Satan's temptations. Rather, He wielded the Scripture as His sword and refuted all of Satan's lies.

However, the lesbian, gay person or bisexual person who acts on his sexual temptation by engaging in sexual conduct outside of the context of heterosexual, monogamous marriage does, in fact, engage in sin. At the very least, the conduct constitutes fornication, and it may also constitute other sins, such as adultery or incest. The transgender person who mutilates his body also commits sin. 1 Corinthians 6:19-20 teaches:

> [D]o you not know that your body is a temple of the Holy Spirit within you, whom you have from God? You are not your own, for you were bought with a price. So glorify God in your body.

In contrast to a homosexual or a bisexual person, who may be subject to sexual temptation but without acting on such temptation, a transgender person has, simply by virtue of changing his gender, undertaken an act. The person can be judged for the act rather than merely for being subject to temptation. The question then becomes whether the act of, for example, having perfectly healthy breasts removed in order for a woman to self-identify as a man, or having one's penis surgically removed in order for a man to self-identify as a woman, is sin.

The Bible has much to say on this question. Paul writes that "your bodies are temples of the Holy Spirit, who is in you, whom you have received from God? You are not your own; you were bought at a price. Therefore, honor God with your bodies" (1Co 6:19). Paul teaches that our bodies are not our own. Indeed, we were not created for our own pleasure or desires. A man who is unhappy with being a man and a woman unhappy with being a woman must recognize that they were created by God for His purposes, not for their own desires.

To remove perfectly health parts of one's body may constitutes a form of self-mutilation that is prohibited in the Bible. The Levitical law states, "'Do not cut your bodies for the dead or put tattoo marks on yourselves" (Lev 19:28). Deuteronomy 14:1 commands not to "cut yourselves or make any baldness on your foreheads for the dead." While these injunctions are associated specifically with practices for the dead, the overarching principle of refraining from self-harm applies more globally. We find that self-harm in the Bible is associated with demon possession, as was the case of the man who lived in the tombs and who "would cry out and cut himself with stones" (Mark 5:5).

Therefore, SHC is correct that being LGB is not necessary sin. However, there is a line that is crossed with the transgender person who actively undergoes surgery to attempt to change his gender. Here, there is actual conduct that may be subject to judgment.

Regarding the claim that if being LGBTQ were a sin, it would be forgiven, the same can be said for every other sin of the Bible. However, just because sin is forgiven does not mean we should continue sinning. As Paul writes in Romans 5:21-6:2:

> ... just as sin reigned in death, so also grace might reign through righteousness to bring eternal life through Jesus Christ our Lord. What shall we say, then? Shall we go on sinning so that grace may increase? By no means! We are those who have died to sin; how can we live in it any longer?

D. THE IDEA OF MULTIPLE GENDER VARIANTS IN THE BIBLE

St. Hugh Church argues that the Bible supports the idea of multiple gender variants:

> All people, including LGBTQ individuals, were created in God's image: "So God created humankind in his image, in the image of God he created them; male and female he created them." (Genesis 1:27, NSRV) The use of the two primary genders in this passage is likely a "merism", a figure of speech by which a single thing (in this case, humanity) is referred to by a phrase that lists several of its parts, but does not list all components. In the other creation passages, day and night are specified, but not twilight; seas and land are mentioned, but not creeks or marshes; vegetation on land but no reference to algae. This passage also indicates that God is not limited to a single gender.

There are multiple issues with this interpretation. First, it is based on a distorted presentation of the book of Genesis. For example, SHC argues that because Genesis mentions only "vegetation on land," but without making a "reference to algae," it is equally possible that God created people who are neither male nor female, but Genesis failed to mention these people when stating "male and female he created them." However, Genesis *does* mention the algae. It is included in "every living thing with which the water teems" mentioned in Genesis 1:21.

Yet even if SHC were correct in that Genesis 1 were not intended to enumerate every living thing that God created and, therefore, this does not mean that God created non-male and non-female persons any more than it means that God created leprechauns, or any other thing not mentioned explicitly in the Bible.

The fact that God created mankind and then issued a command to "[b]e fruitful and increase in number" (Gen 1:28) is clear evidence that He created males and females and that heterosexuality was within the inherent and intended design, since homosexual couples are incapable of reproduction.

St. Hugh Church goes on to argue that non-gender conforming characters who did not behave according to traditional gender roles or that were not physically typical of men or women are found throughout the

Bible. SHC gives the following examples of men in the Bible that have feminine qualities:

- Jacob, who preferred to be with his mother at home, enjoyed cooking and was smooth-skinned, in contrast to his brother, who was hairy and preferred to hunt and be outdoors (Gen 25)
- Joseph, Jacob's son, who was given an "ornate robe" by his father (Gen 37:3), which SHC characterizes as a feminine garment.
- The man carrying a water jar, whom Jesus indicated would take the disciples to the room for his last supper and who was doing work that was normally done by women.

There are multiple issue with SHC's arguments. First, SGH fails to distinguish between a man who might possess a trait, such as smooth skin, or who undertakes an act, such as carrying a water jar, that is traditionally ascribed to women, on the one hand, and a member of the modern LGBTQ+ community who self-identifies as with a gender different from his biological gender or who attempts to changes his gender through medical intervention. There is a fundamental difference between a man who changes a diaper or feeds a crying baby, on the one hand, and a man who calls himself a woman and undergoes sex reassignment surgery.

Second, SHC's argument about Jacob's gifting of a garment to Joseph is misleading. SGH argues that "the Hebrew word used here for the robe (*ketonet passim*) is used elsewhere to mean 'the kind of garment the virgin daughters of the king wore' (2Sa 13:18)." In fact, the term used in Genesis 37:3 (Strong's Number H3801 for the Hebrew כֻּתֹּנֶת / kutōnet) occurs 29 times throughout the Scriptures. The term is gender-neutral and can refer to a garment worn by either a man or a woman. In fact, in five instances (Exo 28:4; Exo 28:40; Exo 29:5; Exo 39:27; Lev 8:13), it refers specifically to a garment to be worn by Aaron or his sons, the male priests of Israel.

St. Hugh Church goes on to cite the following examples:

- Deborah (Judges 4-5), a judge of Israel, acting as a prophet and military leader at a time when women were treated like property and valued by the number of children they could bear.

- Hegai, the eunuch in charge of the palace women in the story of Esther, who helped Esther to become queen.
- Ebed-Melech, a eunuch who saved the life of the prophet Jeremiah (Jer 38).

It is unclear what exactly SHC is attempting to prove by citing these examples. Regardless, what these examples demonstrate is the value that the Bible gives women, who are given special leadership roles (the case of Deborah) and the fact that eunuchs played important roles in the Bible (the case of Hegai and Ebd-Melech). Never does the Bible suggest that women in the Bible underwent gender transitioning or self-identified as men, nor is the forcible castration of men, effectively turning them into eunuchs with a weakened sex drive, is promoted.

E. BIBLE VERSES THAT HAVE BEEN USED TO CONDEMN LGBTQ PEOPLE

St. Hugh Church identifies Bible verses that have been used to condemn LGBTQ people and argues that these verses, when properly understood, do not, in fact, prohibit "loving, consensual same-sex relationships" or "people living as their authentic genders" (*i.e.*, men who self-identify as women and vice versa). We will examine each of SHC's arguments and refute them in turn.

1. Sodom and Gomorrah Were Destroyed Due to a Lack of Hospitality

St. Hugh Church argues as follows:

> Genesis 19:1-13 The Sodom & Gomorrah story is preceded by examples of Abraham and Lot being very welcoming to strangers. The lack of hospitality and the desire to do violence to the visitors were considered grave transgressions, regardless of the gender of the visitors. The reference in Jude 1:7 to "strange flesh" likely refers to the fact that the angels they wanted to assault were not human. "Now this was the sin of your sister Sodom: She and her daughters were arrogant, overfed and unconcerned; they did not help the poor and needy." (Ezekiel 16:49)

The Scripture does not support the view that a lack of hospitality was the cause of the destruction of Sodom and Gomorrah. In arguing that a lack of hospitality was at the root of the problem, SHC selectively quotes from Scripture in an incomplete and misleading manner. If we examine the relevant verses in question in their entirety, it is clear that the sexual immorality of the inhabitants of Sodom—and in particular the attempted forcible homosexual rape of Lot's guests—was the cause of its destruction. SGH quotes only Ezekiel 16:49, but leaves out Ezekiel 16:50, which indicates that it was not *only* arrogance, gluttony and unconcern for the poor and needy that was the cause of Sodom's destruction. The verses state:

> Eze 16:49 "'Now this was the sin of your sister Sodom: She and her daughters were arrogant, overfed and unconcerned; they did not help the poor and needy.
>
> Eze 16:50 They were haughty and did detestable things before me. Therefore I did away with them as you have seen.

The key here is that there were "detestable things" that Sodom committed, in addition to Sodom's arrogance, gluttony and lack of concern for the poor and needy, that was the cause of its destruction. What were these "detestable things"? They were Sodom's sexual immorality and sexual perversion, as evidenced by its inhabitants' attempted rape of Lot's guests. Lot pointed out the wicked nature of the inhabitants' scheme to rape his guests:

> Gen 19:5 They called to Lot, "Where are the men who came to you tonight? Bring them out to us so that we can have sex with them."
>
> Gen 19:6 Lot went outside to meet them and shut the door behind him
>
> Gen 19:7 and said, "No, my friends. Don't do this wicked thing.

The scheme was so detestable that Lot offered the men his two virgin daughters in lieu of his guests:

> Gen 19:8 Look, I have two daughters who have never slept with a man. Let me bring them out to you, and you can do what you like with them. But don't do anything to these men, for they have come under the protection of my roof."

In other words, Lot offered the intruders the means to perpetrate one detestable act in order to avoid a second, even more detestable, act.

Jude similarly makes clear that it was sexual immorality, not inhospitality, that was the cause of the destruction of Sodom and Gomorrah:

> Jude 1:7 In a similar way, Sodom and Gomorrah and the surrounding towns gave themselves up to *sexual immorality* and *perversion*. They serve as an example of those who suffer the punishment of eternal fire.

St. Hugh Church selectively quotes from this verse to muddy Jude's clear message prohibiting sexual immorality. First, SHC ignores entirely Jude's reference to sexual immorality, focusing only on the reference to "perversion." In fact, Jude states that Sodom and Gomorrah "gave themselves up to [both] sexual immorality and perversion" (Jude 1:7).

Second, SHC opts for a translation of G2087 (ἕτερος / heteros) and G4561 (σάρξ / sarx) found in the KJV translation of the Bible, which renders the terms as "strange flesh," rather than of more modern translations, such as the NIV, which renders the terms as "perversion." This translation permits SHC to back away from the argument that sexual immorality and perversion were the cause of Sodom and Gomorrah's destruction and that instead, it was the attempted rape of angels—not homosexuals—that was the cause.

This interpretation lacks grounding. First, it would require ignoring entirely the reference in Jude 1:7 to "sexual immorality," which was indisputably a part of the sin that brought on Sodom and Gomorrah's destruction. Both the NKJV and the NIV include the reference to "sexual immorality"; the KJV translates the term as "fornication." Either way, it is indisputable that the inhabitants of Sodom and Gomorrah engaged in sexual behavior that contravened God's moral code.

Second, SHC's proposed interpretation that Sodom and Gomorrah were destroyed for giving themselves up to sexual relations with celestial beings has no logical or scriptural support. There is no instance in the Bible that reports that the inhabitants of Sodom and Gomorrah had sexual relations with celestial beings. Genesis 19:5 discusses an instance in which the inhabitants attempted to have sexual relations with the angels, but they never succeeded in doing so.

Regardless of whether the Greek term ἕτερος σάρξ is translated as "perversion" or "strange flesh," it is necessary to point out the term σάρξ (flesh) is often used in the Bible to refer to not just any flesh, but specifically to male flesh. The Blue Letter Bible includes the following definitions of the term: "the body of a man," "the sensuous nature of man" and "the animal nature." In this light, it is difficult to argue the Sodom and Gomorrah were destroyed due to inhospitality rather than due to sexual immorality.

Not a single verse in the Bible states that Sodom and Gomorrah were destroyed as a result of inhospitality. It would indeed be incongruous that God would assign such a drastic punishment—the complete obliteration of both cities—for such a relatively inconsequential sin, one that is not even mentioned in the 1 Corinthians 6:9-10 list of grave sins that prohibit entry into the kingdom of God.

2. Prohibition on Homosexual Relations in Leviticus 18:22

St. Hugh Church teaches that Leviticus 18:22 ("Do not have sexual relations with a man as one does with a woman; that is detestable"), when properly understood, is intended to prohibit not homosexual relations, but incest:

> Leviticus 18:22 The NIV translation of this verse reads: "Do not have sexual relations with a man as one does with a woman; that is detestable." The literal translation of the original Hebrew, however, is "And with male you shall not lie lyings woman." The word translated as "lyings" is found elsewhere only in Genesis 49:4, where it refers to incest. In Leviticus, this verse comes in a list of prohibitions against having sex with family members, so it is reasonable to conclude that it is a prohibition against incest.

SHC is mistaken on multiple fronts. First, the literal translation of Leviticus 18:22 is not:

> And with male you should not lie lyings woman.

Ch. 4. Does the Scripture Affirm the LGBTQ Community?

Rather, it is as follows[4]:

Not lie with mankind lying [bed] woman.

Second, the word translated as "lying down" (מִשְׁכָּב / miškāḇ / H4904) does not occur only in Leviticus 18:22 and Genesis 49:4, as SHC states. Rather, it occurs 46 times in 44 verses throughout the WLC Hebrew. The term is generally used to mean "bed" or "lying."

Third, while it is true that the reference to H4904 in Genesis 49:4 has some nexus to incest, incest is not the central focus of the term. Genesis 49:4 states the following about Reuben, Jacob's firstborn son:

> Gen 49:4 Turbulent as the waters, you will no longer excel, for you went up onto your father's bed [H4904 / מִשְׁכָּב / miškāḇ], onto my couch and defiled it.

---

[4] See the following breakdown of Leviticus 18:22:

KJV	Strong's Ref.	Hebrew	Transliteration	Meaning
Thou shalt not	H3808	לֹא	lō'	Not
lie	H7901	שָׁכַב	šāḵaḇ	lie / lie down
with	H854	אֵת	ēṯ	with / together
mankind,	H2145	זָכָר	zāḵār	mankind / male
as with	H4904	מִשְׁכָּב	miškāḇ	lying down / act of lying / bed
womankind:	H802	אִשָּׁה	'iššâ	wife / woman / female
it	H1931	הוּא	hû'	that / same / which
is abomination.	H8441	תּוֹעֵבָה	tôʻēḇâ	abomination / idolatry

The reference to Reuben's going up to his father's bed in Genesis 49:4 relates back to Reuben's sexual relationship with his father's concubine, Bilhah, as recounted in Genesis 35:22:

> Gen 35:22 While Israel was living in that region, Reuben went in and slept with his father's concubine Bilhah, and Israel heard of it.

However, the term miškāḇ (מִשְׁכָּב / H4904) does not necessarily relate to incest. It simply relates to lying down, especially for sexual contact. Such sexual contact can be within the context of incest, but it can also be within the context of any other sexual relations, whether heterosexual, homosexual or involving pedophilia, pederasty, bestiality, adultery or other forms of fornication. In fact, of the 46 instances in which the term miškāḇ (מִשְׁכָּב / H4904) appears in the Old Testament, only Genesis 49:4 has any nexus to the idea of incest. The rest simply refer to beds or lying down (for sexual contact), and two instances (Leviticus 18:22 and Leviticus 20:13) point very clearly to prohibited homosexual relations.

Finally, if Leviticus 18:22 were in fact referring to incest rather than to homosexual relations, it would be rendered redundant and unnecessary, as previous verses already given much more specific instructions on prohibited incestual relations.

3. Paul's Condemnation of Homosexuality in Romans 1:26-27

St. Hugh Church argues that Paul's condemnation of homosexuality in Romans 1:26-27 is no condemnation at all. In fact, Paul is saying nothing of homosexuality as understood in the modern social context as a monogamous sexual relationship between two loving, committed, same-sex partners. Rather, Paul is condemning other harmful acts within the context of Roman culture at the time SHC writes:

> Romans 1:26-27 Here, Paul is condemning the sinful and harmful acts he perceives in Roman culture at the time. Since same-gender and non-heterosexual attractions are natural, this condemnation is not directed at LGBTQ people.

Here, SHC is partially correct. In fact, Paul *is*, as SHC states, "condemning the sinful and harmful acts he perceives in Roman culture at the time." But what SHC misses entirely is that these harmful acts are homosexual relations. We know this because Paul states in Romans 1:26-27 the following:

> Because of this, God gave them over to shameful lusts. Even their women exchanged natural sexual relations for unnatural ones. In the same way the men also abandoned natural relations with women and were inflamed with lust for one another. Men committed shameful acts with other men, and received in themselves the due penalty for their error.

Paul states without equivocation that women who exchange natural sexual relations for unnatural ones (i.e., by burning with lust for other women) and men who abandon natural relations with women in exchange for unnatural ones (i.e., by burning with lust for other men) commit shameful acts and errors that generate consequences. These consequences are not rewards or blessings. Rather, they are a "due penalty for their error." Clearly, then, the exchange of natural relations for unnatural ones following a burning lust for one another is a sin that comes with a penalty.

St. Hugh Church counters this interpretation by stating that because "same-gender and non-heterosexual attractions are natural, this condemnation is not directed at LGBTQ people." In other words, despite what Paul clearly states about homosexual relations, not only in Romans, but elsewhere as well, including in 1 Corinthians and in 1 Timothy, such relations are not in fact sinful because they are "natural." Presumably, by "natural," SHC means that homosexuals do not choose to be attracted to others of the same sex. Rather, these desires are inherent, or what SHC calls "natural." Therefore, they cannot be sinful because they do not arise out of a choice.

This backwards reasoning stands against everything that the Scriptures teach about sin and temptation. If we accept SHC's reasoning, then we can equally conclude that Paul cannot possibly mean in 1 Corinthians 6:10 that the drunkard is a sinner who cannot enter the Kingdom. Rather, he must be talking about some other "sinful and harmful acts he perceives in Roman culture at the time" because the drunkard's desire for alcohol is "natural." He does not choose to be tempted by alcohol. Rather, by drinking alcohol to the point of drunkenness, he is simply acting on his "natural" desires.

The same can be said of the adulterer. He does not choose his desires or temptations. If he could, he would of course choose not to be tempted by the idea of sexual relations with his neighbor's wife. The desires come to him without his volition. Therefore, they are natural, and by acting on them, he is simply acting based on nature and so Paul's condemnation of adulterers cannot be directed at adulterers.

You can see why this reasoning is convoluted and fallacious. Temptation can be characterized as "natural" in the sense that they come to us by virtue of our fallen human nature. But there is a fundamental difference between being subjected to temptation, which every human being—including Christ himself—must endure, and voluntarily taking a decision to act on temptation, whether that decision is to engage in homosexual relations, to drink to the point of drunkenness, to eat to the point of gluttony, to engage in adultery, fornication, bestiality or any other form of sexual immorality, to worship idols, to steal, to slander or to swindle.

4. 1 Corinthians 6:9 and 1 Timothy 1:9-11

a. St. Hugh Church's Argument

Next, St. Hugh Church argues that the condemnations of homosexuality in 1 Corinthians 6:9 and 1 Timothy 1:9-11 are not actually referring to homosexuality at all. Rather, the term "homosexual" is a mistranslation of the original Greek, which in fact referred to men who sleep with enslaved male prostitutes, not men who sleep with other men in committed, loving relationships. SHC writes:

> 1 Corinthians 6:9 and 1 Timothy 1:9-11 The NIV translations of these verses read, respectively: "Or do you not know that wrongdoers will not inherit the kingdom of God? Do not be deceived: Neither the sexually immoral nor idolaters nor adulterers nor men who have sex with men …" and "We also know that the law is made not for the righteous but for lawbreakers and rebels, the ungodly and sinful, the unholy and irreligious, for those who kill their fathers or mothers, for murderers, for the sexually immoral, for those practicing homosexuality …"

The words translated as "homosexuals" and "men who have sex with men" more accurately translate to "men who sleep with enslaved male prostitutes". The word "homosexual" is not found in the Bible in translations written prior to 1948, implying that it was likely added as a result of the translators' own prejudices.

The full verses discussed by SHC are as follows:

> 1Co 6:9 Or do you not know that wrongdoers will not inherit the kingdom of God? Do not be deceived: Neither the sexually immoral nor idolaters nor adulterers nor *men who have sex with men*
>
> 1Co 6:10 nor thieves nor the greedy nor drunkards nor slanderers nor swindlers will inherit the kingdom of God.
>
> 1Ti 1:9 We also know that the law is made not for the righteous but for lawbreakers and rebels, the ungodly and sinful, the unholy and irreligious, for those who kill their fathers or mothers, for murderers,
>
> 1Ti 1:10 for the sexually immoral, for those *practicing homosexuality*, for slave traders and liars and perjurers—and for whatever else is contrary to the sound doctrine.

b. St. Hugh Church's Fallacies

St. Hugh Church is partially correct and partially incorrect and mislead. To start, only one of the verses of the NIV in question—1 Timothy 1:10, uses the term "homosexual." The text of 1 Corinthians 6:9 refers to "men who have sex with men" and is thus unequivocal in its prohibition of sodomy, regardless of whether the term "homosexual" or "homosexuality" appears. However, for the sake of argument, we will assume that both terms use the word "homosexual" and will demonstrate that even if this term were used, SHC's argument would nonetheless lack validity.

St. Hugh Church is correct that English-language translations of the Bible only began to use the word "homosexuality" in translations of 1 Corinthians 6:9 and 1 Timothy 1:9-10 in 1958. However, this is not a reflection of a change in the church's understanding of the verses. It is not as though prior to 1958, the church believed the verses to prohibit sexual relations with enslaved male prostitutes and then, suddenly, in 1958, a segment of the church hostile to homosexuals managed to change the texts in order to reflect their prejudices against homosexuals. Rather, the texts were always understood to prohibit homosexual relations, but there was no term for "homosexuality" at the time of the earliest English translations of the time. In fact, it was only in 1864 that homosexuals were declared as a distinct class of individuals. Before this declaration by the German social scientist Karl Heinrich Ulrichs, homosexual acts were simply considered to be unnatural behaviors. After the declaration, the concept of homosexuality was introduced into social science. It took time—decades—for the idea to catch on and for the English language to adopt a term to describe the group. Prior to the twentieth century, "homosexual" was not a term used in English parlance. As the word "homosexual" became more common in English parlance, it was ultimately introduced into literature, writing, and ultimately, into translations of the Bible. The late use of the word "homosexuality" should thus not be used as evidence that earlier translations of the Scriptures did not condemn homosexual acts; rather, it serves only as evidence that it took time for the modern term for the behavior was used and ultimately incorporated into modern translations of the Bible.

Because heterosexuals were not known as a distinct group during the time of Paul and Moses, there was no word in Hebrew or Greek that referred to homosexuals. According to the Oxford English Dictionary, the first reference of the term "homosexual" in the English language appeared in C. G. Chaddock's 1892 translation of Krafft-Ebing's *Psychopathia Sexualis* III 255. The word simply was not used prior to that time. Thus, it is natural and expected that the term "homosexual" would not appear until English language translations of the mid-1900s. Yet although the term "homosexual" does not appear in earlier editions, the idea of "lying with a man as a man lies with a female" (Lev 18:22) is clearly banned in even the older English translations of the Scriptures.

Because the idea of homosexuality as an identity group only developed at the end of the Nineteenth Century, the word "homosexual" did not appear until the nineteenth century and was not popularized in the English language until the Twentieth Century. Given this history, it is no surprise that the term "homosexual" did not appear in English translations of the

New Testament until the middle of the twentieth century. Language is dynamic, and as words come into existence, written texts will come to incorporate them.

Therefore, although the idea of a "homosexual" as an identity class or distinct group inclined towards sexual relations with the same gender did not exist in the days of Paul and Moses, the sexual behaviors in which homosexuals engage did exist and were clearly prohibited in the Scriptures.

c. History of the Term "Homosexuality"

Although translations of the Bible prior to 1958 did not in fact use the word "homosexual," the idea of sexual relations with members of the same sex does appear in the pre-1958 scriptural translations. The use of the term "homosexual" does not reflect a sudden shift in society's prejudice against homosexuals; it is simply the same idea expressed using a different term. For example, several translations use the term "sodomy" or "sodomites" when translating 1 Corinthians 6:9 and 1 Timothy 1:10. Young's Literal Translation (1862) uses the term "sodomites" in 1 Corinthians 6:9 as well as in 1 Timothy 1:10; the Darby Translation (1890) uses the same term when translating 1 Timothy 1:10. Clearly, if sodomy is banned, then at least male-to-male sexual intercourse was also intended to be banned.

Most of the other pre-1958 translations use the term "abusers of themselves with mankind" or derivations thereof. For 1 Corinthians 6:9, the King James Version (1611) uses "abusers of themselves with mankind"; the Darby Translation (1890) uses "abuse themselves with men"; and the American Standard Version (1901) uses "abusers of themselves with men." For 1 Timothy 1:10, the American Standard Version (1901) uses "abusers of themselves with men." The King James Version uses "them that defile themselves with mankind" (1611).

d. Meaning of the Term "Abuser of Mankind"

The Middle English Dictionary was compiled in 2001 as a comprehensive analysis of lexicon and usage for the period 1100-1500

AD. According to this Dictionary, the first definition of the term abuse ("abusen") is "(a) To misuse (sth.) ... (b) to abuse (sb.) sexually (as by incest, sodomy, prostitution)." Thus, the older translations that use the term "abuse" would necessarily prohibit male homosexual acts where sodomy is involved.

The Oxford English Dictionary, like the Middle English dictionary, also includes the term "misuse" in the definition of the term "abuse." The second definition of "abuse" is "[w]rong or improper use, *misuse*, misapplication, perversion. *spec.* The non-therapeutic or excessive use of a drug; the misuse of any substance, esp. for its stimulant effects" (emphasis added). According to the Middle English dictionary, the second definition of the term "misuse" is to "To misuse (parts of the body, their function or beauty) sexually; to debauch (a woman); *to use (a man or woman) homosexually*" (emphasis added). Thus, homosexual conduct is implicated in the older translations of the Bible that used the term "abuse" or "abuser" of mankind.

Of course, the term "abuser" can mean much more than homosexual in this context. It can be one who "use[s] (a man or woman) homosexually," just as it can mean a pervert or one who misuses the function or beauty of the body in a non-homosexual way (*e.g.*, rape, pedophilia, etc.). Yet the point here is that SHC's argument—*i.e.*, the appearance of the term homosexual only in the later translations of the Bible demonstrates a shift from previous editions—is flawed. The idea of homosexuality is encompassed in the phrases used by previous translations, yet because the word "homosexual" did not exist at the time, they were forced to use a broader term—"abuse of mankind" or a term that equates male-on-male sexual contact—"sodomy."

e. Conclusion

In conclusion, it is natural that the term "homosexual" would not have been used in the Bible until the twentieth century, since it only came into

Ch. 4. Does the Scripture Affirm the LGBTQ Community? 63

existence in the late nineteenth century. It is similarly appropriate that the terms "abuser" and "abuse," and "misuse" would have been used in the earlier translations to signify the same thing, and that the Wycliffe Bible, published centuries before "abuser" and "misuser" came to refer to homosexuals, would have instead used "they that do lechery with men" to refer to the same concept.

5. Jesus' Reference to Eunuchs in Matthew 19:12

a. Overview

St. Hugh Church, relying on Jesus's words in Matthew 19 with respect to Eunuchs who were "born that way," argues that God created more than two genders, that Jesus did not condemn gender variance and, therefore, Christians should not limit themselves to a binary understanding of gender. SHC writes:

> Matthew 19:4 "Haven't you read," [Jesus] replied, "that at the beginning the Creator 'made them male and female'?" In the same section, in verse 12, Jesus says, "For there are eunuchs who were born that way, and there are eunuchs who have been made eunuchs by others—and there are those who choose to live like eunuchs for the sake of the kingdom of heaven." It is evident that Jesus was aware that gender variance existed, and he does not condemn it.

The full verses discussed are as follows:

> Mat 19:4 "Haven't you read," he replied, "that at the beginning the Creator 'made them male and female,'
>
> Mat 19:5 and said, 'For this reason a man will leave his father and mother and be united to his wife, and the two will become one flesh'?
>
> Mat 19:6 So they are no longer two, but one flesh. Therefore what God has joined together, let no one separate."
>
> Mat 19:7 "Why then," they asked, "did Moses command that a man give his wife a certificate of divorce and send her away?"
>
> Mat 19:8 Jesus replied, "Moses permitted you to divorce your wives because your hearts were hard. But it was not this way from the beginning.
>
> Mat 19:9 I tell you that anyone who divorces his wife, except for sexual immorality, and marries another woman commits adultery."

> Mat 19:10 The disciples said to him, "If this is the situation between a husband and wife, it is better not to marry."
>
> Mat 19:11 Jesus replied, "Not everyone can accept this word, but only those to whom it has been given.
>
> Mat 19:12 For there are eunuchs who were born that way, and there are eunuchs who have been made eunuchs by others—and there are those who choose to live like eunuchs for the sake of the kingdom of heaven. The one who can accept this should accept it."

b. Response

St. Hugh Church fundamentally misunderstands Jesus, who states, "there are eunuchs who were born that way, and there are eunuchs who have been made eunuchs by others—and there are those who choose to live like eunuchs for the sake of the kingdom of heaven." Jesus's reference to "eunuchs" must be understand within the cultural context of the time. He is not referring to men or women who voluntarily remove their sexual organs or who choose to identify with a gender other than their biological gender. Rather, he is referring to the Greek term εὐνοῦχος / eunouchos (G2135), which according to the *Outline of Biblical Usage* can be used to mean any of the following:

> I. a bed keeper, bed guard, superintendent of the bedchamber, chamberlain
>
> A. in the palace of oriental monarchs who support numerous wives the superintendent of the women's apartment or harem, an office held by eunuchs
>
> B. an emasculated man, a eunuch
>
>> i. eunuchs in oriental courts held by other offices of greater, held by the Ethiopian eunuch mentioned in Ac. 8:27-39.
>
> C. one naturally incapacitated
>
>> i. for marriage
>>
>> ii. begetting children
>
> D. one who voluntarily abstains from marriage

There are three types of eunuchs mentioned by Jesus in Matthew 19:12 and found throughout the Bible:

Ch. 4. Does the Scripture Affirm the LGBTQ Community?

- 1. Eunuchs "who have been made eunuchs by others." They have been emasculated by others involuntarily. These are generally servants in a royal court or palace who are emasculated in order to remove the temptation of having sexual relations with the ruler's wives or concubines. They do not voluntarily remove their sexual organs in order to identify with the opposite gender;
- 2. Eunuchs "who choose to live like eunuchs for the sake of the kingdom of heaven." As with the first category, they do not voluntarily remove their sexual organs. Rather, they resist their sexual desires and choose to abstain from marriage and begetting children in order to dedicate themselves to the kingdom of God. They do not self-identify with the opposite gender, nor do they engage in homo- or heterosexual relations. Rather, they are abstinent;
- 3. Eunuchs "who were born that way." These are individuals who are naturally incapacitated for marriage and begetting children, either because they are infertile, impotent or have some other defect in their reproductive organs. Jesus is not referring to members of the modern LGBTQI+ community who are born with perfectly-healthy reproductive systems but choose to surgically remove these organs when undergoing gender reassignment surgery, those who choose to self-identify with a gender that differs from their sexual organs or those who choose to dress in clothing of a gender other than their biological gender.

While it is true that Jesus does not condemn any of the eunuchs he specifically refers to (those who are emasculated for their service in royal courts, those who opt for abstinence in order to serve the kingdom of God and those who are born infertile or impotent), He says nothing about members of the modern LGBTQ+ community.

6. Cross-Dressing Deuteronomy 22:5

a. Overview

St. Hugh Church argues that the Bible contains no actual prohibition on cross-dressing. Rather, the injunction in Deuteronomy 22:5 is a prohibition on combatants' pretending to be women and on civilians' pretending to be combatants. SHC writes:

Deuteronomy 22:5 "A woman must not wear men's clothing, nor a man wear women's clothing, for the Lord your God detests anyone who does this." The word translated as "clothing" here, *keli*, is translated elsewhere as "armor", and the word translated as "man", *geber*, actually means "warrior". This implies a prohibition against intent to deceive by pretending to be a warrior, or for a warrior to deceive by disguising himself as a woman.

b. Response

St. Hugh Church's proposal that Deuteronomy 22:5 is intended to prohibit civilians from pretending to be warriors and warriors from pretending to be women makes little sense in the biblical context for multiple reasons, including those discussed below.

a. If the intent were to prohibit perfidy rather than cross-dressing, God would have been clearer

If this were the intent of Deuteronomy 22:5, then God could have denoted the message much more clearly. Rather than state, "a woman must not wear men's clothing, nor a man wear women's clothing," which implies a prohibition on cross-dressing, He could have clearly stated, "a civilian must not deceive by wearing warriors' clothing, nor a warrior by wearing women's clothing." Yet God said no such thing.

b. If the intent were to prohibit warriors from wearing women's clothing, then how were female warriors expected to dress?

If God's intent was to prohibit warriors from wearing women's clothing, then how were female warriors expected to dress? The Bible depicts several female warriors, including Deborah, who was a judge[5] of Israel, and Jael, a heroine who delivered Israel from the army of King Jabin of Canaan in the Book of Judges. If SHC's interpretation of Deuteronomy 22:5 were correct, then these women would have been expected to cross-dress as men. Not only is this contrary to Hebrew practice, but is contrary to the most natural interpretation of Deuteronomy 22:5, which is intended to prohibit, not promote, cross-dressing.

---

[5] The judges of Israel served as military leaders prior to the monarchy.

c. SHC's argument regarding the appearance of the words keli and geber is flawed

SHC's argument regarding the appearance of the words *keli* (normally translated as "clothing") and *geber* (normally translated as "men") is incorrect.

The word *keli* (כְּלִי / H3627) is translated into English versions of the Bible in a variety of ways. In some cases, it is rendered as "weapons" (Gen 27:30), "stuff" (Gen 31:37, 45:20; Exo 22:7), "instruments" (Exo 25:9), "vessel" (Lev 11:33, 11:34) and "thing" (Lev 13:49). Given the wide range of these definitions, the meaning can be summarized in its essence as referring to any thing that is prepared for a particular purpose. This meaning is consistent with the definition given to it by Strong's Definitions (1890):

> something prepared, i.e. any apparatus (as an implement, utensil, dress, vessel or weapon):—armour(-bearer), artillery, bag, carriage, furnish, furniture, instrument, jewel, that is made of, one from another, that which pertaineth, pot, psaltery, sack, stuff, thing, tool, vessel, ware, weapon, whatsoever.

This definition is reflected in many English translations of the Bible, including the KVJ ("The woman shall not wear that which pertaineth unto a man") and the NKJV ("A woman shall not wear anything that pertains to a man").

Moreover, SHC's proposed interpretation of Deuteronomy 22:5 does not take into account the second half of the prohibition, which states that a man should not wear a woman's "clothing" or "garment." Here, the term used for "clothing" or "garment" is the Hebrew *śimlâ* (שִׂמְלָה / H8071), which, unlike the earlier Hebrew term *keli*, is unequivocal in its meaning of "wrapper, mantle, covering garment, garments, clothes, raiment, a cloth" (*Outline of Biblical Usage*). Unlike the term *keli*, it is not given a general definition that can be interpreted to mean anything that is prepared, which it is clothing or armor. In this light, it is logical to read Deuteronomy 22:5 creating parallel obligations for both men and women. Just as men are not to wear women's "garments," so to are women not to wear men's garments.

Finally, with respect to the translation of *geber* (גֶּבֶר / H1397), while the term can be used to refer to a "warrior," its primary meaning refers to a "man." When used as "warrior," it is used to emphasize a man's "strength or ability to fight" (*see Outline of Biblical Usage*). *Strong's Definitions* defines the term as:

> properly, a valiant man or warrior; generally, a person simply:—every one, man, × mighty.

The term appears 65 times in 64 verses in the Old Testament. In all of these instances, it is translated as "man" or "men" in the KJV. It is not translated as "warrior" in any instance of the KJV. In the verses in which the term appears, the idea of a warrior is not stated or implied by the context. Examples include (NKJV):

> Exo 12:37 There were about six hundred thousand *men* on foot, besides women and children.
>
> Psa 37:23 The steps of a good *man* are ordered by the Lord, And He delights in his way.
>
> Psa 40:4 Blessed is that *man* who makes the Lord his trust, And does not respect the proud, nor such as turn aside to lies.
>
> Pro 20:24 A *man's* steps are of the Lord; How then can a man understand his own way?
>
> Jer 23:9 I am like a drunken man, And like a *man* whom wine has overcome, Because of the Lord, And because of His holy words.

As can be seen, none of these instances have any nexus whatsoever with combat or acting as a warrior.

c. Conclusion

We can therefore conclude that SHC's argument that Deuteronomy 22:5 is intended to prohibit pretending to be a warrior or for a warrior to pretend to be a woman—rather than prohibiting cross-dressing—is without merit.

CHAPTER 5. WHAT THE BIBLE SAYS—AND DOESN'T SAY—ABOUT HOMOSEXUALITY

A. INTRODUCTION

In "What the Bible Says - And Doesn't Say - About Homosexuality," Dr. Mel White argues that the Hebrew and Christian Scriptures, when correctly understood, neither condemn nor prohibit homosexual relationships between two loving, committed partners. The apparent prohibitions of sodomy and other homosexual acts in the Old Testament are intended not as injunctions from God, but rather, as reflections of societal tastes and preferences. In any event, the prohibitions and societal preferences of the Old Testament have no place in the new covenant of grace, and therefore should have little bearing on the conduct of contemporary Christians. As for the apparent prohibitions of homosexual conduct in the New Testament, these are mostly based on mistranslations that misunderstand the original text. The term "homosexual" used in Paul's Epistles has no modern English equivalent, and is best rendered as the sexual exploitation of "effeminate call boys" by old men, not homosexuality between two men or two women in committed, loving relationships. Only in translations rendered after the mid-twentieth century did the term "homosexuality" begin to erroneously appear as a reflection of societal prejudices against homosexuals.

First, it must be conceded that Dr. White does make some strong points, such as his argument that the word "homosexual" in 1Corinthians 6:9 and 1 Timothy 1:10 first only appeared in English translations as "homosexual" in 1958. In other areas, however, Dr. White's pamphlet is based on broad assumptions and a rejection of the divine inspiration of the Scriptures.

B. MISUNDERSTANDING THE DIVINE INSPIRATION OF THE SCRIPTURES

Looking at the Old Testament's apparent injunctions against homosexual relations, Dr. White holds that we "miss what these passages say about God when we spend so much time debating what they say about sex." He goes on to examine the condemnations of same-sex relations in the Old Testament, such as Leviticus 18:22[6,7] and Leviticus 20:13.[8] Dr. White argues that to read these as condemnations or prohibitions of homosexual relations is a misinterpretation, for these passages are not intended as absolute statutes written by God on how men and women should treat and relate to one another; rather, they represent a "holiness code," or "list of behaviors that people of faith find offensive in a certain place and time." These statutes reflect a Jewish culture that found same-sex unions to be offensive.

Dr. White here commits several errors. First, he repeats constantly that these injunctions against homosexual relations represent a code that the Jews found offensive, as though this code is nothing more than a list of preferences of the Jewish people. He characterizes this code to a pact to which he bound himself as a high school student: "I don't drink, smoke, or chew, or go with girls who do." Dr. White misses, however, the first premise of orthodox Christianity: the Hebrew Scriptures were written by God through inspired prophets, not by individuals seeking to record cultural preferences. The Scriptures that Dr. White quotes were given to Moses by God: "Then the LORD spoke to Moses, saying [Lev 18:1] ... You shall not lie with a male as with a woman [Lev 18:22]" and again in

---

[6] All Scriptures are taken from the New International Version® (NIV) (copyright © 1973, 1978, 1984 Biblica. All rights reserved. The "NIV" and "New International Version" trademarks are registered in the United States Patent and Trademark Office by Biblica), unless otherwise indicated.

[7] "You shall not lie with a male as one lies with a female. It is an abomination."

[8] "A man who sleeps with another man is an abomination and should be executed."

Leviticus 20: "Then the LORD spoke to Moses, saying [Lev 20:1] ... If a man lies with a male as he lies with a woman, both of them have committed an abomination [Lev 20:13]." Thus, when homosexuality is prohibited in the Jewish law, we must read this as God's injunction, not as man's injunction.

Yet Dr. White claims just a few paragraphs later that an abomination in the Hebrew Scriptures is a behavior that "people in a certain time and place consider tasteless or offensive." Here, Dr. White essentially ignores the preface "Then the LORD spoke to Moses ...," and can only do so if he denies that the Scriptures are divinely inspired, perfect and complete. This denial of the divine inspiration of Scripture can only be true if Leviticus 18:22 ("You shall not lie with a male as one lies with a female") were written by Jews of the time reflecting their cultural preferences. Yet if this were the case, then Leviticus 18:1 ("the LORD spoke to Moses, saying ...") cannot be true. It must be fabricated if God is not the author. And if Dr. White believes the verse to be fabricated, then in what way does he "take the Bible seriously"? Certainly not as an orthodox Christian who believes the Bible to be the perfect, unaltered and true Word of the living God.

Dr. White's discussion of Genesis 38:9-10 similarly reveals this problem. The verses state that Onan "spilled his seed on the ground," and that "the thing which Onan did displeased *the Lord*" (emphasis added). It does not state that the thing displeased the Jewish writers of the text; it states clearly that it displeased the Lord. Yet this is not the point that Dr. White takes from the text. Rather, he interprets the text to mean that for "Jewish writers of Scripture," masturbation or the interruption of coitus was "an abomination (and one worthy of death)." He clearly misses that if the Bible is the true and unaltered Word of God, it was God who was offended by Onan's act.

If Dr. White took the Scripture seriously (in the sense of believing it to be true), then there would be no question as to what the Jewish writers of Scripture found to be displeasing or offensive. When the Scripture says that "the thing which Onan did displeased the Lord," the discussion would end there, with no discussion of whether the spilling of semen was displeasing to the Jewish author, since the text does not state "the thing which Onan did displeased this author." He would accept with faith that the Scripture, divinely inspired by God and wholly true, displeased God; otherwise, he would have to believe that the Bible is at best partially accurate and partially corrupted by human experience, culture, the preferences of the writers, etc.

Of course, there are verses in the Scripture that support the notion that homosexuality was judged by the Jews as sinful. For example, in the book of Judges, when the men of the city came to the master of the house demanding that he bring out his guest that they may "know him carnally" (Jdg 19:22), the master implored them not to "act so wickedly" (Jdg 19:23). If all of the Scripture's references to homosexuality were expressed in this way as the private judgment of individual actors, then there would be no reason to object to Dr. White's arguments. Yet the Bible states clearly that homosexuality gravely displeased God in addition to these individual actors.

C. THE OLD TESTAMENT LAW AS INAPPLICABLE TO MODERN SOCIETY

1. Overview

Dr. White's next argument is that the Old Testament Law was abrogated by Jesus and Paul and is no longer applicable to Gentile Christians. Dr. White writes, "Jesus and Paul both said the holiness code in Leviticus [which appears to condemn homosexuality] does not pertain to Christian believers." The "holiness code" is, according to Dr. White, largely irrelevant and outdated, and includes prohibitions on, among other things, "round haircuts [Lev 19:27], tattoos [Lev 19:28], working on the Sabbath [Exo 23:12], wearing garments of mixed fabrics [Lev 19:19], eating pork or shellfish [Lev 11:7-12]," or playing with pigskins, as in football (Lev 11:8 prohibits eating the flesh of swine or touching their carcasses). Dr. White is correct here in some respects but his statements are overbroad and thus inaccurate.

2. The Old Testament Law with Israel

It is first important to understand the nature of the Old Testament Law. It was given to Moses by God as part of a Covenant between God and the nation of Israel. It was never intended as binding on all peoples. When God became man through Christ, a New Covenant was established through which all who profess Christ as Savior would be saved. The Covenant was not restricted to any one people or ethnicity. Nor was it based on obedience to the Old Testament Law. Just as the Old Testament established a Covenant by Law, the New Testament formed a Covenant through Grace.

3. Was the Old Testament Law Abrogated?

This should not, however, be taken to mean that the Old Testament Law was abrogated. Christ states that "until heaven and earth disappear, not the smallest letter, not the least stroke of a pen, will by any means disappear from the Law until everything is accomplished" (Mat 5:18). The Law continues to stand as the means to Salvation, yet because all have fallen short of the Law and have sinned (Isa 53:6; Rom 3:10), God has provided a gate to Salvation through Christ's fulfillment of the Law in his perfect, sinless life and Atonement. Christ thus proclaims: "Do not think that I have come to abolish the Law or the Prophets; I have not come to abolish them but to fulfill them" (Mat 5:17).

It is important to discern the difference between the letter of the Law and the spirit of the Law. God is concerned with the spirit of the law. Christ was displeased when the Pharisees and scribes placed all of their attention on the letter of the law while ignoring the spirit of the law. For example, he accused the scribes and Pharisees of paying "tithe of mint and anise and cummin, and [yet neglecting] the weightier matters of the law: justice and mercy and faith (Mat 23:23), and then says, "These you ought to have done, without leaving the others undone" (Mat 23:23). It thus does not suffice that one obey the outward dimensions of the Law; it is more important that he fulfill the spirit of the Law.

4. The Spirit of the Law

It therefore cannot be said, as Dr. White writes, that "Jesus and Paul both said the holiness code in Leviticus does not pertain to Christian believers." What can, however, be said is that the Old Testament Law applies to Christians in a different way. Christians are lifted to a higher standard. They are expected to obey the Law while not ignoring the weightier matters of the Law: justice and mercy and faith. The spirit of the Law becomes paramount over the letter of the Law. Thus, Christians are prohibited not only from the sin of murder, but also from being angry at one's brother (Mat 5:22). Similarly, it is not enough that Christians refrain from adultery; they must also refrain from even looking at a woman lustfully, for such is the equivalent of "adultery of the heart" (Mat 5:28).

5. How Then Can We Be Saved? The Council of Jerusalem

Of course, no one but Christ can proclaim a sin-free life that has fulfilled both the letter and the spirit of the Law. This is why God has given the gift of grace. The Council of Jerusalem recognized and affirmed this. When some were teaching that the Gentile converts to Christianity were required to undergo circumcision and to follow other precepts of the Old Testament Law, the Council concluded that the Gentile converts were required only to "abstain from food sacrificed to idols, from blood, from the meat of strangled animals and from sexual immorality" (Act 15:29).

It would be easy to read this Council as having abrogated all of the Old Testament Law, with the exception of the four cited prohibitions. Yet such a rash reading would overlook the message of the Gospel. Taken with Christ's earlier-cited teachings, the Council did not intend to abrogate the Old Testament Law, but rather, to acknowledge that it was through God's Grace, not through the Law, that one could be saved. Rather than burden the Gentile converts with laws by which even the Jews could not abide, the Council decided to make only a small fraction of the law binding and to allow the lives of the converts to be guided to good fruit through the Holy Spirit.

The Council thus held that the Gentile converts would not be under the Old Testament's circumcision requirement. This is not because the Old Testament Law was abrogated. Rather, the disciples recognized Christ's teaching that what is paramount is the spirit of the Law. Christ seeks not outward, physical circumcision, but circumcision of the heart. With a heart turned towards God, the Old Testament circumcision requirement is fulfilled.

This is the approach that believers must take towards the Old Testament Law. The Church understood that the Laws still applied, but in a different way. Whereas in the Old Covenant, circumcision was an outward physical sign, in the New Covenant, it is of the heart. Just as the Old Testament Law is a forerunner of New Testament Grace, so too is outward, physical circumcision a forerunner to inward, spiritual circumcision.

Thus, one cannot write off so quickly the Old Testament Laws against homosexuality, just as one cannot write off those against round haircuts and the like. Each of these laws speaks to man's good, to his relationship with God and to his relationships with other people. Though the content of many of these laws may appear to be outdated and inapplicable to modern day society, the spirit behind them continues to work towards man's good.

For example, Leviticus 27-28 states: "Do not cut the hair at the sides of your head or clip off the edges of your beard. Do not cut your bodies for the dead or put tattoo marks on yourselves." These four prohibitions most likely deal with mourning rites: "The hair-cutting of verse 27 is probably associated with the skin-cutting in verse 28, and both were related to specific pagan rituals having to do with the dead. The description of the cuts made on the body 'for the dead' in verse 28 offers explicit support for this interpretation."[9] The ban on these rites cannot be understood without acknowledging the Jews' flirtation with idolatry: Leviticus 27-28 intends to ban idolatrous rites. The spirit of these laws is fulfilled when the believer worships the one true God and flees idolatry. Though the letter of the Law was given to Israel within a specific content, the spirit of the law continues to apply today. The same can be said of the

---

[9] Rob Bowman, "Gay Marriage and the Haircut Argument," *in The Religious Researcher*, 11 Dec. 2009, available at http://www.religiousresearcher.org/2008/12/11/gay-marriage-and-the-haircut-argument/.

entire code of the Old Testament; as Christ said with His own words, he came not to "abolish the Law or the Prophets ... but to fulfill them" (Mat 5:17).

6. Distinguishing the Different Forms of Law

Christians must thus discern the spirit of the Laws of the Old Testament in order to understand how they continue to apply in their lives. The Old Testament's sacrificial offering of animals had been fulfilled by the cross, because Christ's body was the final and ultimate sacrifice. The sacrifice of animals is thus no longer required of Christians, because the final sacrifice was made. Many of the hygienic laws of the Old Testament applied to Jews at a time when modern technologies did not exist. Although some of the dietary laws and prohibitions against mixed fabrics may appear outdated to modern ears, the spirit behind these Laws, which focus on being a good steward of one's body, continues to apply.

7. "Sexual Immorality" as Homosexual Relations

Yet even if Dr. White were correct and all of the laws outlined in the Old Testament were abrogated, homosexuality would still be prohibited on the basis of Acts 15:29, which requires believers to "abstain from ... sexual immorality" (Act 15:29). As we will see below, sexual immorality to the writers of the New Testament included homosexual relations, because the writers of the New Testament repeatedly condemned homosexuality. The Council, in placing a continued banned on sexual immorality, reaffirmed and preserved the Old Testament's prohibition on homosexual relations.

D. THE BIBLE: A BOOK ABOUT GOD OR "HUMAN SEXUALITY"?

Dr. White's next argument states that the biblical verses dealing with human sexuality speak *not* to the sexual relations between men and women, but rather, to God's holiness, since "the Bible is a book about God, not about human sexuality." These passages should therefore not be read as prohibitions on human sexual behavior.

1. The Copernicus Argument

Dr. White first points to the heliocentric cosmology that some passages of the Bible appear to point towards (e.g., Joshua 10:13). He states that theologians of Copernicus's day, including Martin Luther, condemned Copernicus's heliocentric cosmology because they failed to understand that Joshua 10:13, like the rest of the Bible, is about *God, not* about astronomy. Because the Bible is not meant to deal with questions as to whether the earth revolves around the sun or vice versa, we should not condemn the theories of astrologists such as Copernicus that appear to contradict verses such as Joshua 10:13, because these verses in reality do not deal with astrology; they deal with God. Dr. White then draws a parallel to those verses that appear to condemn homosexuality: these passages are about God, not about human sexuality, and we should not take from these verses a blanket ban on homosexual relations.

Dr. White's analysis is flawed in two respects. The first is in its interpretation of Joshua 10:13. Although Dr. White is correct in pointing out that those who read Joshua 10:13 and related passages as evidence against Copernicus's heliocentric cosmology were mistaken in their reading, Dr. White's reading that the passage has *nothing* to do with astrology is similarly flawed. The passage correctly states that the sun stood still for a full day. It is important however to note that this passage describes what was perceived *from the perspective of the people perceiving the event*. To these people, the sun appeared not to move through the sky. This does not mean that the sun normally revolves around the earth, just as the expressions "the sun rose" and "the sun set" do not necessarily mean that the sun actually moves around the earth. Just as the concepts of sunset and sunrise could indicate that the sun stands still and the earth makes a full rotation each day, so too could the idea of the sun moving through the sky indicate the same thing. The fact that certain church authorities at the time of Copernicus interpreted the verse as counter to a heliocentric cosmology does not in itself mean that the verse has nothing to do with astrology or that the sun did not stand still from the human perspective.

2. The Bible Is about God's Holiness, Which Has Implications over the Conduct of Mankind

The second way in which Dr. White's analysis is flawed is that if followed to its natural conclusion, the Christian would deem all of the commandments that govern human relations to be irrelevant. If we conclude like Dr. White that the Bible is a "book about God, not about human sexuality," then we could also state that it is also not about human anger, or human jealousy, or human dishonesty. If one would were to conclude that 1 Corinthians 6:9 dealt only with God, and not human sexuality, why would he not also conclude that Exodus 20:14, which prohibits adultery, was a commandment dealing only with God, and not human sexuality? If all of these commandments, from those given on Mount Sinai to those given in the Sermon on the Mount, do not concern the affairs of men, then they could all be equally ignored.

In reality, the Bible is about God's holiness, and God's holiness has implications over the conduct of mankind because we are created in God's image and are thus commanded to reflect His nature in holy, righteous, pure living. Part of living purely means fleeing sexual immorality. It is no wonder that in the Epistles alone, fornication and other forms of sexual immorality are condemned half a dozen times (1Co 6:9-10; 1Co 6:13b, 18; 1Co 10:6-8; Gal 5:19-21; 1Th 4:3-5; Eph 5:1-3).[10]

E. HOMOSEXUALITY IS ALSO BANNED IN THE NEW TESTAMENT

Dr. White's next focus is on the New Testament. Having argued that the Old Testament's bans on homosexuality were only cultural reflections and that the Old Testament Law was in any case abrogated, Dr. White is faced with the New Testament's bans against homosexual conduct. Here, his principal argument is that homosexuality was never banned in the New Testament; rather, sexually abusive relationships, of which "homosexuality" is a mistranslation, were condemned and prohibited. To

---

[10] The term "fornication" is used in these verses in the King James Version. The term used varies in other translations.

Ch. 5. What the Bible Says—and Doesn't Say—about Homosexuality 79

evaluate whether Dr. White's arguments are persuasive, we will examine the three New Testament verses that he treats: Romans 1:26-27, 1 Corinthians 6:9, and 1 Timothy 1:10.

1. Romans 1:26-27

Romans 1:26-7 states: "For this reason God gave them up to vile passions. For even their women exchanged the natural use for what is against nature. Likewise also the men, leaving the natural use of the woman, burned in their lust for one another, men with men committing what is shameful."

Dr. Mel White, citing arguments made by Dr. Louis B. Smedes, argues that because the homosexuals refused to worship God, God abandoned and gave them up to sexual immorality. Yet he has it backwards; it is not that these men and women succumbed to sexual immorality because they refused to worship God; rather, it is because they engaged in homosexual activities that God abandoned them. It is not that they sank into sexual depravity because they rejected God, but rather, God abandoned them because they engaged in homosexual activity. The text states, "For this reason God gave them up to vile passions. For even their women exchanged the natural use for what is against nature. Likewise also the men, leaving the natural use of the woman, burned in their lust for one another, men with men committing what is shameful" (Rom 1:26-7). "For this reason" refers to the actions of the following sentences: "For even their women exchanged the natural use for what is against nature ..." The text could just as easily read: "Because their women exchanged the natural use for what is against nature ..., God gave them up to vile passions."

Dr. White's interpretation is credible in some respects. Romans 1:23 describes the sins of idolatry of the godless, and is directly followed by, "Therefore God gave them over in the sinful desires of their hearts to sexual impurity for the degrading of their bodies with one another" (Romans 1:24). This makes it appear as though the homosexuality of the godless came about as a result of their own sins. Yet even this interpretation is not favorable to homosexuality: if homosexuality is a state that God delivers the depraved into as a result of their rejection of God, then is homosexuality a state to be desired? Whether it is a sin that causes God's abandonment of the sinner or a state brought about as a result of sin, homosexuality is a state to be avoided. Even if Dr. Smedes is granted his argument, and we conclude that "The people Paul had in mind refused to acknowledge and worship God, and for this reason were abandoned by God. And being abandoned by God, they sank into sexual depravity," then the biblical text is equating sexual depravity with the homosexual exchange of "the natural use for what is against nature," thus equating homosexuality with sexual depravity.

2. First Corinthians 6:9 and First Timothy 1:9-10

a. Introduction and Overview

First Corinthians 6:9 states: "Do you not know that the wicked will not inherit the kingdom of God? Do not be deceived: Neither the sexually immoral nor idolaters nor adulterers nor male prostitutes nor homosexual offenders." 1 Timothy 1:9-10 states: "We also know that the law is made not for the righteous but for lawbreakers and rebels, the ungodly and sinful, the unholy and irreligious, for those who kill their fathers or mothers, for murderers, 10 for the sexually immoral, for those practicing homosexuality, for slave traders and liars and perjurers. And it is for whatever else is contrary to the sound doctrine."[11]

Dr. White argues that these texts, which are often used as evidence of the Bible's condemnation of homosexuality, do not actually refer to homosexuality as we understand it. Rather, they refer to sexually abusive or perverted behavior. Only recently did translations of these texts begin to render the term as "homosexuality."

---

[11] This translation is taken from Today's New International Version. The NIV uses the term "perverts" in place of "homosexuals." Other translations that use "homosexuals" include the New American Standard Bible, the Contemporary English Version, the International Standard Version, God's Word Translation, the Holman Christian Standard Bible, Today's New International Version, and the Modern King James Version. The New Living Translation and the English Standard Version translate the term as men "who practice homosexuality."

b. The Idea of Homosexuality is in the Scriptures, even if the Word "Homosexual" is not

a. Overview

Dr. White is correct in pointing out that starting only in 1958 did English-language translations of the Bible begin to use the word "homosexuality" in translations of 1 Corinthians 6:9 and 1 Timothy 1:9-10. However, it is important to note that it was only in 1864 that homosexuals were declared as a distinct class of individuals. Before this declaration by the German social scientist Karl Heinrich Ulrichs, homosexual acts were simply considered to be unnatural behaviors. After the declaration, the concept of homosexuality was introduced into social science. It took time—decades—for the idea to catch on and for the English language to adopt a term to describe the group. Prior to the twentieth century, "homosexual" was not a term used in English parlance. As the word "homosexual" became more common in English parlance, it was ultimately introduced into literature, writing, and ultimately, into translations of the Bible. The late use of the word "homosexuality" should thus not be used as evidence that earlier translations of the Scriptures did not condemn homosexual acts; rather, it serves only as evidence it took time for the modern term for the behavior was used and ultimately incorporated in modern translations.

Because heterosexuals were not known as a distinct group during the time of Paul and Moses, there was no word in Hebrew or Greek that referred to homosexuals. According to the Oxford English Dictionary, the first reference of the term "homosexual" in the English language appeared in C. G. Chaddock's 1892 translation of Krafft-Ebing's *Psychopathia Sexualis* III 255. The word simply was not used prior to that time. Thus, it is natural and expected that the term "homosexual" would not appear until English language translations of the mid-1900s. Yet although the term "homosexual" does not appear in earlier editions, the idea of "lying with a man as a man lies with a female" (Lev 18:22) is clearly banned in even the older English translations of the Scriptures.

Because the idea of homosexuality as an identity group only developed at the end of the Nineteenth Century, the word "homosexual" did not appear until the Nineteenth Century and was not popularized in the English language until the Twentieth Century. Given this history, it is no surprise that the term "homosexual" did not appear in English translations of the New Testament until the middle of the Twentieth Century. Language is dynamic, and as words come into existence, written texts will come to incorporate them.

Although the idea of a "homosexual" as an identity class or distinct group inclined towards sexual relations with the same gender did not exist in the days of Paul and Moses, the sexual behaviors in which homosexuals engage did exist and were clearly prohibited in the Scriptures.

b. *History of the Term "Homosexuality"*

Dr. White asserts that the use of the word "homosexual" only first appeared in the translations of the Scriptures in 1958, and "that translator made the decision for all of us that placed the word homosexual in the English-language Bible for the very first time." Dr. White then suggests that "the decision ... that placed the word homosexual in the English-language Bible for the very first time" reflects "society's prejudice and [desire to] condemn God's gay children."

I must respectfully disagree. Although the Scriptural translations prior to 1958 did not in fact use the word "homosexual," the idea of sexual relations with members of the same sex does appear in the pre-1958 scriptural translations. The use of the term "homosexual" does not reflect a sudden shift in society's prejudice against homosexuals; it is simply the same idea expressed using different words. For example, several translations use the term "sodomy" or "sodomites" when translating 1 Corinthians 6:9 and 1 Timothy 1:10. Young's Literal Translation (1862) uses the term "sodomites" in 1 Corinthians 6:9 as well as in 1 Timothy 1:10; the Darby Translation (1890) uses the same term when translating 1 Timothy 1:10. Clearly, if sodomy is banned, then at least male-to-male sexual intercourse was also intended to be banned.

Most of the other pre-1958 translations use the term "abusers of themselves with mankind" or derivations thereof. For 1 Corinthians 6:9, the King James Version (1611) uses "abusers of themselves with mankind"; the Darby Translation (1890) uses "abuse themselves with men"; and the American Standard Version (1901) uses "abusers of themselves with men." For 1 Timothy 1:10, the American Standard Version (1901) uses "abusers of themselves with men." The King James Version uses "them that defile themselves with mankind" (1611).

c. *What is the meaning of the term "abuser of mankind" that appears so frequently in the older English translations?*

The Middle English Dictionary was compiled in 2001 as a comprehensive analysis of lexicon and usage for the period 1100-1500 AD. According to this Dictionary, the first definition of the term abuse ("abusen") is "(a) To misuse (sth.) ... (b) to abuse (sb.) sexually (as by incest, sodomy, prostitution)." Thus, the older translations that use the term "abuse" would necessarily prohibit male homosexual acts where sodomy is involved.

The Oxford English Dictionary, like the Middle English dictionary, also includes the term "misuse" in the definition of the term "abuse." The second definition of "abuse" is "[w]rong or improper use, *misuse*, misapplication, perversion. *spec.* The non-therapeutic or excessive use of a drug; the misuse of any substance, esp. for its stimulant effects" (emphasis added). According to the Middle English dictionary, the second definition of the term "misuse" is to "To misuse (parts of the body, their function or beauty) sexually; to debauch (a woman); *to use (a man or woman) homosexually*" (emphasis added). Thus, homosexual conduct is implicated in the older translations of the Bible that used the term "abuse" or "abuser" of mankind.

Of course, the term "abuser" can mean much more than homosexual in this context. It can be one who "use[s] (a man or woman) homosexually," just as it can mean a pervert or one who misuses the function or beauty of the body in a non-homosexual way (*e.g.*, rape, pedophilia, etc.). Yet the point here is that Dr. White's argument—the appearance of the term homosexual only in the post-1957 translations demonstrates a shift from previous editions—is flawed. The idea of homosexuality is encompassed in the phrases used by previous translations, yet because the word "homosexual" did not exist at the time, they were forced to use a broader term.

3. Conclusion

In conclusion, it is natural that the term "homosexual" would not have been used in the Bible until the twentieth century, since it only came into existence in the late nineteenth century. It is similarly appropriate that the terms "abuser" and "abuse," and "misuse" would have been used in the earlier translations to signify the same thing, and that the Wycliffe Bible, published centuries before "abuser" and "misuser" came to refer to homosexuals, would have instead used "they that do lechery with men" to refer to the same concept.

CHAPTER 6. CONCLUSION

In light of the foregoing, we can conclude that the Bible neither promotes, permits nor condones homosexuality, bisexuality or transgenderism. Instead, the only form of sexuality prescribed by the Bible is heterosexuality within the context of monogamous marriage between a man and a woman. Prohibitions of homosexuality are found throughout the Old Testament, including in Genesis, Leviticus and Judges, and the New Testament, including in Romans, 1 Corinthians and 1 Timothy.

Christians must be uncompromising in speaking truth. Yet this does not mean that Christians are to judge or condemn homosexuals. Rather, the proper attitude towards homosexuals should be the same attitude towards any other person: love and compassion. A person who struggles with homosexual temptations is no different from any other person who struggles with sin and temptation. Temptation is common to all of us: "No temptation has overtaken you except what is common to mankind" (1Co 10:13). We must recognize that "all have sinned and fall short of the glory of God" (Rom 3:23). Therefore, we are in no position to judge our brothers and sisters who struggle with homosexuality.

Yet refraining from passing judgment is not the same as accepting homosexuality as an alternative to biblically-sanctioned heterosexual relationships. As Christians, we must love our neighbor and refrain from judging while simultaneously proclaiming truth. This means defending biblical precepts of marriage and sexuality while projecting patience, gentleness and love.

ANNEX 1.
BIBLICAL VERSES DISCUSSING HOMOSEXUALITY

1. **Genesis 19:5-8**

    Gen 19:5-8 They called to Lot, "Where are the men who came to you tonight? Bring them out to us so that <u>we can have sex with them</u>." Lot went outside to meet them and shut the door behind him and said, "No, my friends. <u>Don't do this wicked thing</u>. Look, I have two daughters who have never slept with a man. Let me bring them out to you, and you can do what you like with them. But don't do anything to these men, for they have come under the protection of my roof."

    > Revisionist response: This prohibits rape or attempted rape, not homosexual relations between consenting adults.

2. **Leviticus 18:22**

    Lev 18:22 'Do not have <u>sexual relations with a man</u> as one does with a woman; that is detestable.

    > Revisionist response: This prohibits cultic prostitution, not homosexual relations between consenting adults.

3. **Leviticus 20:13**

    Lev 20:13 If a man has sexual relations with a man as one does with a woman, both of them have done what is detestable. They are to be put to death; their blood will be on their own heads.

    > Revisionist response: This prohibits cultic prostitution, not homosexual relations between consenting adults.

4. **Judges 19:20-25**

Jdg 19:20-25 "You are welcome at my house," the old man said. "Let me supply whatever you need. Only don't spend the night in the square." So he took him into his house and fed his donkeys. After they had washed their feet, they had something to eat and drink. While they were enjoying themselves, some of the wicked men of the city surrounded the house. Pounding on the door, they shouted to the old man who owned the house, "Bring out the man who came to your house *so we can have sex with him*." The owner of the house went outside and said to them, "*No, my friends, don't be so vile. Since this man is my guest, don't do this outrageous thing. Look, here is my virgin daughter, and his concubine. I will bring them out to you now, and you can use them and do to them whatever you wish. But as for this man, don't do such an outrageous thing.*" But the men would not listen to him. So the man took his concubine and sent her outside to them, and they raped her and abused her throughout the night, and at dawn they let her go.

> Revisionist response: This prohibits rape or attempted rape, not homosexual relations between consenting adults.

5. Romans 1:26-28

Rom 1:26-28 Because of this, God gave them over to shameful lusts. Even *their women exchanged natural sexual relations for unnatural ones*. In the same way the men also abandoned natural relations with women and were inflamed with lust for one another. *Men committed shameful acts with other men*, and received in themselves the due penalty for their error. Furthermore, just as they did not think it worthwhile to retain the knowledge of God, so God gave them over to a depraved mind, so that they do what ought not to be done.

> Revisionist response: This only prohibits homosexuality performed as part of pagan idolatrous rituals and the Isis cult in Rome, not homosexual relations between loving, consenting adults.

6. 1 Corinthians 6:9-10

1Co 6:9-10 Or do you not know that wrongdoers will not inherit the kingdom of God? Do not be deceived: Neither the sexually immoral nor idolaters nor adulterers *nor men who have sex with men* nor thieves nor the greedy nor drunkards nor slanderers nor swindlers will inherit the kingdom of God.

> Revisionist response: This prohibits male prostitution and pederasty, not homosexual relations between consenting adults.

7. 1 Timothy 1:9-11

1Ti 1:9-11 We also know that the law is made not for the righteous but for lawbreakers and rebels, the ungodly and sinful, the unholy and irreligious, for those who kill their fathers or mothers, for murderers, for the sexually immoral, *for those practicing homosexuality*, for slave traders and liars and perjurers—and for whatever else is contrary to the sound doctrine that conforms to the gospel concerning the glory of the blessed God, which he entrusted to me.

> Revisionist response: This prohibits male prostitution and pederasty, not homosexual relations between consenting adults.

www.ingramcontent.com/pod-product-compliance
Lightning Source LLC
LaVergne TN
LVHW051153080426
835508LV00021B/2595